Phil —

My hope is that you
find some value within
these pages and enjoy
some of the stories!

Josh

PRAISE FOR LESSON 1

The difference between a successful team and one that fails rests entirely on the performance of the leader. If you want to be a great leader, you need to learn and practice leadership. There is no better way to learn leadership than to listen to those who have deep experience leading people. John VanDusen has been there. He has been on the front lines of leadership and has learned what it takes to succeed in the most challenging environments. In Lesson 1, you will gain practical, hands-on knowledge that will allow you to become a leader who makes a difference in the lives of your followers. Become a leader worth following by reading this book!

Jon S. Rennie
Bestselling author of All in the Same Boat: Lead Your Organization Like a Nuclear Submariner, former U.S. Navy Nuclear Submarine Officer, President & CEO of Peak Demand Inc.

I really enjoyed reading Lesson 1: Leveraging Leadership in Everyday Life for a few reasons. Number one, like everyone else, I have a busy schedule and it was easy to pick up, read, get a great takeaway and put back down for tomorrow's lesson. #2 - I'm a simple guy, and it was written in simple, plain, easy to understand examples and stories that are applicable to my life. #3 This book challenged many of my ideas about leadership. I love leadership books, and I took away a lot to immediately apply to my own leadership role as a principal.

Chris Fore
Eight Laces Consulting, Veteran Athletic Director, Football Coach, Principal, President of the California Coaches Association

Lesson 1 provides great leadership principles that span all types of organizations and teams. John VanDusen uses his experiences in the Army, as a classroom teacher, and as a coach to explain themes of strong leadership skills that are vital to any successful organization. By using practical examples of leadership successes and pitfalls, Lesson 1 offers sound advice no matter where your leadership falls on an organizational chart. By utilizing the image of a round room with four sides, readers are challenged to think about the various pressure points and time constraints they may experience in their own leadership journey and focus on how they can serve those they lead in the best way possible. Overall, Lesson 1 provides readers valuable insight into the paradox that all leaders face when they are forced to prioritize when everything is a priority.

Jay R. Dostal, Ed.D.
Father, Educator, 2016 Nebraska Principal of the Year,
2021 Arkansas Principal of the Year

John VanDusen hit the nail on the head with Lesson 1, Leveraging Leadership in Everyday Life. This book made me realize just how often we are called upon to be leaders. Not just at work but in our everyday life. John has created a distinctive approach in prioritizing each one of his leadership lessons in a way that is unique to the individual reader. Additionally, John does an excellent job sharing his personal journey. You almost feel as though you are walking in his shoes; you feel his emotions. This book is more than just a leadership guide, it's a book that reminds you just how precious life is. John makes you understand that leadership fluctuates and he does an excellent job providing you with the necessary tools to deal with the impossible challenges that may arise. This book truly encourages you as you navigate your own personal leadership journey.

Dominic Armano
Assistant Principal, Proud Educator

John first off I would like to say congratulations on your book and thank you for your service to our nation and youth. I'd like to say wow, wow, wow, what a great read!! John you owned every word, lesson, and page in your book; you left no questions unanswered in reference to the topics you discussed. I would recommend your book to any audience and can wait to add it to my list of recommended readings. Anyone who reads this book will certainly walk away a better leader or future leader. Reading your book helped me realize that there are leaders at every level and in all professions that face very similar challenges whether it's work, family, coaching, organization etc; however, with the proper balance there are ways to dedicate the appropriate level of time and attention needed to be successful. Your real world experiences and solutions regarding how to deal with certain situations are priceless and eye opening. One of my favorite topics referenced trusting our subordinates and exploiting their strengths to improve their weaknesses is something we can all do a better job at. Thank you for sharing and investing in all leaders and future leaders who will certainly gain valuable knowledge and skills after reading your book. I have no doubt your book will be a huge success and provides sound advice and methods for balancing the things most important in our lives such as our family, careers, self development, extracurricular activities, friends, and coworkers to name a few. Best of luck JVD and again outstanding job brother.

John W. Moore Jr.
Supervisory Police Officer; U.S. Department of the Treasury
Major, U.S. Army Reserves

Life lessons. We experience them every moment of each day. John offers leadership in how we choose to embrace the good, the bad, and the ugly. He guides us through his journey. It is heartfelt, completely authentic, and sincere. His passionate honesty allows opportunities for introspection and evaluation, followed by the ability to embrace inevitable discomfort to stay true to the inner self. John brings inspirational enlightenment with a generous balance of vulnerability and humor. The clarity that I have gained from his unique perspective has prepared me to refresh and reconfigure my blueprint as I step into understanding my purpose with deeper intention.

Jillian DuBois
Elementary Educator, Author, Illustrator

There is a reason why John VanDusen's new book is called Lesson 1. When you read it, that reason will become crystal clear to you. Every single lesson is equally as important as the last. Take, for example, a piece of advice found in the chapter on asking stupid questions: "We preach solid communication plans but then there is a stigma for trying to clarify the communication. Don't let that be you."

A teacher, coach, and soldier, VanDusen has written a gem on leadership that will benefit you whether you're in a leadership position currently or planning to be in one someday. It is a book you don't want to miss. If you do, you'll already have missed the first lesson.

Dr. Jeff Prickett
High School Principal, 2021 Illinois High School Principal
of the Year, Podcast Host: The Principal Leadership Lab

John VanDusen has successfully taken his years of experience in the army as an officer and combined it with his experiences as a teacher and football coach to provide us all with valuable lesson on life and leadership. John very succinctly provides a series of leadership lessons that, if you wade into this book with an open mind, I guarantee will make you a better leader and person. Leadership is a skill that takes practice and continued learning and John provides a great series of lessons. Kudos to John for putting into words the lessons so many of us could use to improve our effectiveness.

Kenneth Dilg
U.S. Army Colonel (Retired)

John's lessons are all ones that cause you to reflect and look at not only your leadership differently but life differently. His stories give you an appreciation for each lesson and how they can help move you forward. Lesson 1 is a lifetime of learning, and each lesson that John breaks down takes you back to the basics. This book is for anyone looking to move forward in all aspects of their life.

Melissa Wright
Mathematics Teacher, Author, Renaissance Advisor,
President - New Brunswick Student Leadership
Association

Throughout the book, John gives a refreshing and human perspective into leadership that all walks of life can relate to in some way, shape or form. Using a number of real life situations and experiences, any reader that picks up Lesson 1 will see the steps one can take to become a leader in their own lives. By the end of the book, John really drives home the message: Anyone in any role can be a leader, but you must be willing to lead!

Brady Grayvold
College Football Coach & former UW-Whitewater football
player

John's straightforward and transparent approach to writing is welcoming and encouraging for all those who are striving to become better leaders in their sphere of influence. Whether you've been a leader for years, are just beginning in a new leadership role now, or feel that you will be called to a position of leadership in the future, this book is for you!

Coach Kurt Hines
Husband, father, grandfather, friend, teacher, coach

"If wise men remain quiet, while they are not injured, brave men abandon peace for war when they are injured, returning to an understanding on a favorable opportunity: in fact, they are neither intoxicated by their success in war, nor disposed to take an injury for the sake of the delightful tranquility of peace." History of the Peloponnesian War, Book 1

Moral impartiality for considerations and ethical logic and utilitarian traditions, integrity are often times ignored by leaders and decision makers, stated by Thucydides. Reading the practical authenticity and self awareness in John VanDusen's writing, his life journey as a servant leader, his commitment and motivation to leader development are inspiring. In this book he is influencing one's assumptions and perceptions in their social norms settings, enabling self-awareness parameters underlying a foundation for social skills, traits and attributes in path for growth and becoming a better leader.

Professor Tirdad Daei
Professor of Organizational Leadership

In Lesson 1, John has written a refreshingly honest and simple look at leadership that transcends roles or job titles. He builds on his extensive backgrounds in education and the military to give us 21 practical ways to lead in our everyday lives, lessons that can all be "lesson 1" depending on the situation. Reading this book will help you, and the people around you, more effectively become the humble and effective servant leaders that our world needs today.

Chris Woods
Teacher & STEM Nerd, Author of Daily STEM

I thoroughly enjoyed this book. Mr. VanDusen has managed to create an interesting read on leadership. I found it clever, sincere, and enlightening. The book held my attention from beginning to end. The author validates himself in the introduction, describing the many hats he has worn during his lifetime: soldier, family man, teacher, coach. The lessons themselves are a valuable reiteration of what leaders look like. Lessons which are sometimes taken for granted are highlighted by quotes and explanations. What strikes home, though, is the way VanDusen sprinkles in his own personal stories and anecdotes in each chapter. We see a certain validation, whether it's describing the decision to reroute Blackhawk helicopters during a firefight in Iraq or taking accountability for a blown timeout call in a high school football game. The personal stories allow this book to deviate from the run of the mill, sleep inducing lectures on leadership. I highly recommend Lesson 1, not just for aspiring leaders, but for anyone wishing for an illuminating and interesting read.

Jon Lorenzoni
English Teacher, Basketball/Soccer Coach

In his book, Major John VanDusen provides excellent leadership lessons and life experiences. Whether it be a parent passing this valuable insight on to their children or anyone coming into a leadership position, VanDusen displays the roadmap for being a successful leader. For those already in a management or leadership role, this book serves as a solid reminder and gut check of valuable leadership qualities one must maintain to provide efficient leadership.

Jonathan French
U.S. Army Sergeant First Class (Retired)
Project Manager/Civil Engineer, Hockey Coach, Father

If you're looking for THE book on leadership, then the search stops with Lesson 1 by John VanDusen. John combines practical examples from his military background and educational leadership experience to deliver a product that is practical, to the point, and easy to put into practice. Put simply, this book is a roadmap to success in leadership and also life.

Chris Young
Strategic Learning Coordinator - Southern Hancock
Schools

Practical leadership lessons are at your fingertips with this wonderfully written book by John VanDusen. Drawing from his own experiences, VanDusen honestly shares insightful and applicable tips from the perspective of the roles he's played in his family, as a teacher, coach, and in the army. Walk alongside as VanDusen reveals leadership ideas to elevate your effectiveness throughout each and every day. If you're looking to improve as a leader, this is the book for you!

Livia Chan
Elementary Head Teacher, Author, and Digital Content
Editor for the Teach Better Team

John VanDusen uses his experiences from his life, coaching, and the military to provide the reader with valuable leadership strategies that can easily be applied at any level. His lessons are real and easy for the reader to understand and relate to. Whether you have been in a leadership role for years, or you're looking to dip your toes into the leadership waters, this book is a must have for anyone wanting to improve their leadership skills.

Robert F. Breyer
Author, Leadership Consultant, Podcast Host, and School Principal

John's experiences as a teacher, coach, and Army officer present a wide array of leadership lessons that are incredible on their own. However, John does masterful work in weaving these lessons seamlessly with one another and making them applicable across the board, not just in the classroom, the field/court, or the military. John's 21 leadership lessons are a must for anyone in education to embrace, whether a new or experienced teacher, an administrator, a coach, etc. Take charge of your leadership skills through Lesson 1!

Kyle Anderson
Special Education Teacher, Author, Podcaster, Presenter

LESSON 1

LEVERAGING LEADERSHIP IN EVERYDAY LIFE

JOHN VANDUSEN

FOREWORD BY
**MAJOR GENERAL
SYLVESTER CANNON**

LESSON 1: LEVERAGING LEADERSHIP IN EVERYDAY LIFE

TABLE OF CONTENTS

FOREWARD

Military commander, Teacher, and Coach are the titles Major John VanDusen has held both singularly and collectively. Rarely do you encounter an individual who has held these important positions in their lifetime and has excelled in each of them. With these important positions coupled with the unique life experiences that go along with them, Major VanDusen has captured the essence of leadership in our everyday lives.

This is absolutely one of the best books on leadership I have ever read. Not only will you thoroughly and completely enjoy reading Major John VanDusen's book on leadership, but you will also become captivated by his real-life experiences that continue to make him a great leader. His background and training as an educator have not only enabled him to provide us with a pure understanding of the art of leadership, but the science behind it as well.

Major John VanDusen worked for me as the Commander of the 144th Military Police Company while I commanded the 226th Maneuver Enhancement Brigade - Kabul Base Cluster in Afghanistan from 2013 to 2014. During this time period, the United States and the Coalition forces were still very actively engaged in Operation Enduring Freedom, responding to multiple "green on blue" incidents as well as mass casualty events.

While in this contested environment, interactions between small unit leaders and the higher levels of the military structure were not unusual; they were commonplace. However, I don't think Major VanDusen or I could envision what the future would hold for the leaders we were working with, and surrounded by, during this time period. General John Dunford, the ISAF

Commander, would eventually become the Chairman of the Joint Chiefs of Staff. Lieutenant General Mark Milley, the III Corps Commander, will eventually become the Chief of Staff of the Army and the Chairman of the Joint Chiefs of Staff. MG James McConville, the 101st Division Commander during this time, would eventually become the Chief of Staff of the Army.

During Major VanDusen's service as a Company Commander in war-torn Afghanistan, his life experiences and leadership skills were not only enhanced by these high-level leaders on the ground during his tour of duty but also by the daily interactions with his soldiers and the coalition partner countries.

Reading this book on leadership will be well worth your time and effort. You will fundamentally enjoy the straight-forward writing style of this evolved leader as well as learn more on the subject of leadership. This is a great guide to exercising your leadership skills on a daily basis.

Major General Sylvester Cannon
Commanding General
167th Theater Sustainment Command

INTRODUCTION

I believe our experiences shape how we see the world and how we expect others to see it as well. When I go to a conference featuring a keynote speaker, I want to know as much about the speaker as possible before I walk in the door. I feel the same way about an author when I read a book.

With that in mind, here is the short version of who I am:

John VanDusen

- Graduate of Kingsford High School (GO FLIVVERS!) in Michigan's Upper Peninsula (U.P.)

- Bachelor of Arts Degree in elementary education from Northern Michigan University

- Graduate of Ohio University (Bobcats, not Buckeyes) with a Master's of Science Degree in recreational science

- Eighth grade history teacher at Kingsford Middle School

- Enlisted in the Army National Guard at 17

- Deployed to Iraq as a platoon leader

- Deployed to Afghanistan as a Company Commander

- Instructor for the Command and General Staff Officer College

- Football coach

- Former tennis and basketball coach

- Married with a son from a previous marriage

- Worst sinner I know and not strong enough to save myself (this is why I have a savior in Jesus Christ, He deserves all the glory and fame for what He did for me on the cross)

Now, if you would like to know more about me as a person before you dive into the leadership lessons, here is the long version:

I was born to Carl and Tracy VanDusen in February of 1982. My parents were both from the Upper Peninsula of Michigan and were each raised modestly, at best. Both of my parents had a strong work ethic and an appreciation for everything they had because there were times when they had nothing. Not me, I had absolutely everything! I did not have everything in terms of things. I had a loving family who made me a priority. I had two dogs who were like siblings. I had grandparents who loved me and looked after me. I had an example of leadership in my own house that I would not come to realize until I was in my late twenties.

The first person to teach me leadership, my dad, is easy to understand. When I was born, my dad had just returned from a deterrent patrol on the USS Stonewall Jackson, a ballistic missile submarine out of Charleston, South Carolina. His job was to keep the nuclear reactors inside one of the most advanced weapons of war running flawlessly, and he did so flawlessly. Mistakes were not tolerated 700 feet below the polar ice cap, playing hide and seek with Russsian Akula class, hunter-killer submarines. My dad retired from the Navy after 23 years as a Command Master Chief and had recently returned from a deployment where his ship was called on to fire tomahawk missiles into Bosnia-Herzegovina. The Sailors upon the USS Normandy performed perfectly and, the missile strikes so eloquently documented on CNN, were partly due to my dad and the relentless training he imposed on the Sailors aboard the CG-60. I am sure time underwater led to his pursuit of perfection in drills. Anything less than perfection was not tolerated when perfect was possible.

The second person to teach me leadership did not pound its way through my thick skull until I was much older. I had no idea how much my mom did and purposely did not do for our small family. As a young boy, my dad would deploy on submarines for months at a time, and I was not old enough to understand what was going on. I did not have time to think about it because while dad was gone I was enrolled in swimming lessons, T-ball, cub scouts, 4-H, and everything else you can think of for a young boy on the west coast to be involved in.

When dad was home, however, it was time to be a family. All of those extracurricular activities only happened when dad was gone to sea. Most of this was orchestrated by my mother. As far as I knew, we were the closest knit family that ever existed. My mother was a genius. I think it is probably pretty normal for a son to realize that as they enter their thirties.

My mother passed away on January 21, 2017. I was with my parents in their home when she stiffened and became unconscious while sitting in her favorite chair. Because they lived about 12 miles out of town, the State Police took 22 minutes to arrive, and the ambulance took 27 minutes. It was the only time I had performed CPR on a real person and a few things stuck out in my mind. First, you really do break ribs. For some reason this surprised me. Second, the look on the young State Trooper's face when he came bursting through the front door with the AED was of shock and disbelief. My look and language said, "What are you doing? Get down here!"

I lost seven men in Iraq and to this day I remain almost emotionless around death. However, this was my mom. I was feeling emotions I physically could not hold back. My mom was declared deceased as soon as the ambulance reached the hospital. The most brilliant woman I had ever met passed away with no warning. My sincerest thanks to the Michigan State Police and the EMTs who arrived on the scene and completely took over. You accomplish heroic acts everyday and I am sincerely thankful for the work you do.

A lot of things have shaped me as a person and a leader. The death of my mom may have had the biggest impact on how I view my life. Before my mom ascended to heaven, my life motto was "Life is about Relationships and Experiences." Since she left us, this phrase has become so true to me that I refuse to turn down any experience or healthy relationship.

This mindset shaped the direction of this book. While you read the Lessons remember: life is a precious gift that may be taken at any time. Two other things inspired the text in this book: my time in the Army and being a teacher and coach.

I started writing down the ideas for this book after I had been in the Army for about 15 years. By then, I had served in leadership roles for two combat deployments. My first was to Baghdad, Iraq as a Second Lieutenant where I started as a Platoon Leader with the 46 Military Police Company. When I lost my very best friend and Platoon Sergeant, Jim Priestap, I had a breakdown. After about 20 days of doing various odd-jobs, I was moved to a Platoon Leader position with Echo Company, 1 Battalion, 125 Infantry, callsign: "Hooligan." Going back into combat was by far the best thing that could have happened to me. We saw a lot of combat including some terrible things no one should have to experience, but we experienced them together. Most of us are still fighting battles within our own hearts and minds over things that happened.

In my second deployment, I was the Company Commander for the 144 Military Policy Company, callsign: "Blackhats." There were some familiar faces from my first deployment. First Sergeant

(1SG), Greg Humphrey, was one of them. There was nothing a Soldier could do, say, or think that 1SG Humphrey had not already done, said, or thought himself. He was truly great at his job. My second in command and Executive Officer (XO) was Brice Kerschen. He is an outstanding Army officer, police officer, husband, father, and friend. This deployment was very different in the structure of the organization and the operating environment. As the Company Commander I only had operational control over eight out of 150 Soldiers, most of whom were providing security to other units and bases. It was very frustrating preparing the unit for war then being told to take a backseat and farm out my unit to other organizations. My leadership would not be in conducting Company Level assaults on Taliban strongholds, but rather coordinating with base commanders and other entities to take care of my Soldiers. 1SG Humphrey, First Lieutenant (1LT) Kerschen, and I had become underpaid politicians. However, my interpersonal skills and, dare I say, charm provided top cover to my Soldiers and we had an extremely successful deployment.

I love teaching and I love coaching! My first five and a half years of being a teacher were at the middle school level in L'Anse, Michigan. I had some great teaching partners and learned a lot about being an educator and a member of a community. I took a break from teaching to go to Afghanistan. Upon my return, on orders, I stayed full-time with the Army for another two and a half years.

I was then able to get a job teaching STEM at Kingsford, which I have always called home. Teaching STEM to Pre-K thru 5th grade is a trip. After three years in the STEM classroom, I was finally able to get my dream job: 8th grade U.S. History. Now every day I get to step into the shoes of our founding fathers. It is inspiring to dig into the Declaration of Independence, Constitution, and Bill of Rights almost every day of the first semester.

Coaching is a whole new ball game (see what I did there) when it comes to teaching and leadership. It too has been an amazing experience. For me, the coolest part is teaching students at the middle school level, then coaching them as they get older. Being able to see them progress as athletes, students, and people is a blessing.

While at L'Anse, I coached junior high, junior varsity, and varsity football as well as junior high basketball. I learned volumes of information about coaching for the Purple Hornets. Coaches like Rob Willman, John Jacobson, and U.P. Sports Hall of

Fame coach Jerry Bugni helped me realize what I knew (very little) and how to learn what I did not know (A LOT). I owe a ton to Coach Mark Leaf, the varsity football coach for the Hornets. I was a new guy and maybe a little too intense for my own good, but he brought me on the staff, trusted me, and helped me develop as a coach.

About 20 minutes after accepting the teaching job at Kingsford, Mark Novara, the assistant varsity coach at the time, called and said, "JVD! I heard you just got hired! We need a third coach on our freshman team and you're it. Their practice is at 9:00 tomorrow!" For the next two years I got to coach with the men who coached me, specifically, Jim Myllyla and Chris Hofer. The Flivver Nation is a very special place and I consider myself truly blessed to work alongside some amazing coaches and some even better young men.

THE ROUND ROOM WITH FOUR SIDES

The diagram below helps me visualize how I move through my day using the various leadership lessons outlined in this book. I picture myself in a round room with four sides. It is not as crazy as it sounds. Look at the picture below. Throughout the day, I move around the room giving my attention to different areas of my life. The four big areas, or sides of the room, are family, teacher, coach, and army.

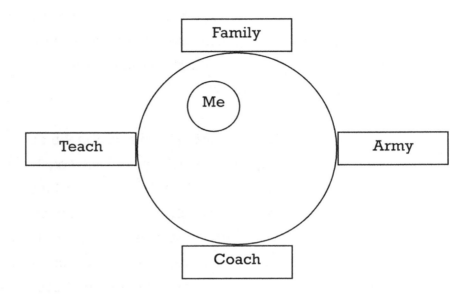

It is very hard to stand in the exact center of the room. All sides are pulling at me for attention. Sometimes I need to ignore one side of the room completely because I am being pulled so strongly toward another side. When I am conducting Army training I am standing on the far right side of the room and am not paying any attention to the teacher side of the room. When I have a break in training, I may be able to call my family or text a fellow coach, but that is about all. On the other side of the room, if I am teaching 25 eighth graders about the Oregon Trail, my Army email sits unopened. On game-day, I am pulled to the coaching side of the room for about four hours and the other parts of the room do not receive my attention.

To help you visualize this, here is a typical Friday through Monday scenario for me in the fall on a drill weekend. On Friday morning, I start on the teacher side of the room and the other sides do not receive any attention. Occasionally, I take a short walk over to the coaching side to make sure my game-plan is laminated or I have the opposing team's roster, but for the most part I stay on the teacher side of the room. Little to no interaction with the family or Army sides occurred.

After school, I quickly walk to the coaching side and prepare for battle. We might be on a bus or in our own locker room, but after school is done it is time to coach and win a football game. Again, the other sides of the room do not receive any attention during that time. I am not any less of a father, teacher, or Army officer, it simply means the football team warrants my full attention.

After the game is over, I move to the family side, say goodbye, then head over to the Army side. The Army side can be relentless. Sometimes I have to drive 500 miles to even get to that side. Sometimes I have to sit on the family side and call the Army side during the week. Sometimes I stay on the Army side for two weeks during annual training, or longer during a deployment to Iraq or Afghanistan. All sides of the room are demanding, but the Army side of the room is cold-hearted about it. This is okay, however, because the people standing on that side with me are some of the best in the world. They walk away from the other parts of their rooms in order to serve a broader purpose.

After spending Friday night through Sunday afternoon on the Army side of the room, I head back over to the loving arms of my family. I do not get to stay there long because Monday morning I am back on the teacher side of the room, trying not to die of dysentery (remember we were learning about the Oregon Trail).

I have thought about moving through my day this way for quite a while. My brain sometimes does a double-take now that my son is old enough to join me on the sidelines of a football game. The family side of the circle is getting pushed toward the coaching side and I like it!

Another interesting aspect of my round room is that I am now a teacher for the Army. For 20 years my teaching job and my Army job could not have been more different. I wore different clothes and spoke a different language. In one job I was teaching pre-teens, in the other I was training adults to close with and kill the enemy with accurate machine gun, rifle, and pistol fire. Now that I am teaching for the Army, it is almost like I am packing up my backpack on Friday from school, going to the other side of the room, and using the same equipment. I just wear an Army uniform instead of a Flivver Football polo shirt. Not much is different between those two sides anymore.

How many sides are in your round room?

HOW TO THINK ABOUT LESSON 1

If you are called upon to be a leader, then lead to the best of your ability. While you are leading, follow Lesson 1. This will mean different things to different people in different situations. However, each of these lessons can be brought to the front of the line depending on the moment.

If you are currently in a leadership position, I challenge you to apply these lessons to the moments of your day. If you are a leader inside of a school system, you have many vertical levels of contact each day and each of them requires a different type of leader. You will deal with students, staff, teachers, principles, parents, superintendents, and school board members each with a slightly different objective. If you are a leader in another organization, you may find your vertical influences are customers, managers, supervisors, and corporate headquarters.

Horizontally you have many different relationships as well, some of which may require you to act in a leadership role. Leading a team of peers is much different than working on a team under a superior, regardless of your organization. Both scenarios can prove to be a tight rope walk, but your balance in leadership skills will keep you from tumbling down.

If you are not in a leadership position at the moment, you are in a perfect position for two reasons. First, you can reflect on previous leadership experiences. By viewing these lessons through the lens of the past, you can review your actions and get a sense of how you might make decisions if placed in that situation again. My second company command was exactly like this. In my humble assessment, I did fairly well in my first command, but when I was asked to take over the Blackhats, I did much better. I learned from my shortcomings and capitalized on my strengths.

Second, you are in a great position to observe your current leaders and the decisions they are making. Notice I used the word observe not judge. This would become painfully clear to me when I was expected to call the offense for the JV Flivver football team. I had been coaching for 14 years at that point, but always on the defensive side of the ball. When it was not my decision to make, I felt I always had the perfect offensive play call. When it was my decision to make, I realized how hard it was to balance down, distance, personnel grouping, etc. I felt like I had never coached football before! You are in a great position to observe. Keep it on the observation level and run the actions and inactions you see through the lessons that follow.

When you first looked at this book, you no doubt noticed that every lesson is lesson one. Each lesson is labeled as lesson one because it is impossible to rank these in an analytical way for your leadership role, whether this is at work or at home. Let me explain by walking you through a typical day.

6:00 a.m.   **At the gym**--Take care of yourself
8:00 a.m.   **Answering emails**--Know when to talk and know when to write
11:00 a.m.   **Staff meeting**--If it is important, get a teacher in front of the group; Ask the stupid question

12:30 p.m.	Lunch--Be yourself; Take care of yourself
2:00 p.m.	Writing plans for your team—Written plans do not get read
3:00 p.m.	Meeting with a team member on a special project--Tell your subordinates how they are doing; Flip the pyramid; Be a servant leader
5:00 p.m.	Fender bender in the parking lot-OWN IT!
6:30 p.m.	Son's piano recital-Be there

At any point throughout your day, you may find one or two lessons to be the most important at that moment. To assume any lesson is more important than another is to ignore the fact that we are dynamic creatures and change tasks, locations, companies, and roles at multiple points during our typical day. This is compounded by the different roles we are asked to play throughout the day: parent, spouse, board member, coach, counselor. The list of demands on us is endless and it changes sometimes by the minute.

Some lessons will prove more useful than others, some you may hardly use at all. You must acknowledge your current situation and the best lesson to use at that moment, realizing it may change rapidly. The leadership skills are the same regardless of where you are standing in the round room, just the method of employment changes.

LESSON 1:
BE THERE

If there was a true Lesson 1 in leadership, this is it. I'm not big on quoting people, but one I rely on is from Colin Powell. Army General Colin Powell did two tours in Vietnam, one as a Captain and one as a Major. He rose to the rank of four-star general and was the youngest Chairman of the Joint Chiefs of Staff from October 1, 1989 to September 30, 1993. He oversaw the invasion of Panama and Desert Storm and also served as Secretary of State for President George W. Bush from 2001-2005. He was a leader on the ground in Vietnam as well as in the Pentagon. He said, "The commander in the field is always right and the rear echelon is wrong, unless proved otherwise."

This is very true in the Army. While in Iraq, when air support showed up, the pilots would only talk to someone on the ground. They understood that it may not always be the commander of the unit, but it was someone who was physically on the ground who could tell them what was going on. As much as the leader "in the rear" thought they knew, they did not know everything in real time.

AIR SUPPORT: Attack Helicopter or Fixed Wing attack aircraft that have their fire directed by troops on the ground. Almost all of the air support I received in Iraq was in the form of AH-64 Apache Helicopters.

There was a night when some of the Iraqis we were supporting got into a gunfight. When we arrived, it was hard to tell what was going on, but we had Apache helicopters overhead. The new landowner, who had only been there a few weeks, was talking to the pilots on their brigade frequency. I was asking, not politely, for their Battalion to give us the helicopters, meaning I wanted them to tell the Apaches our frequency and call sign so we could talk with them. They refused. I switched my radio to the brigade frequency and called the helicopters down to myself. This was frowned upon due to all the other traffic the brigade was monitoring. For a platoon leader to clog up the airwaves with some less than polite language raised some eyebrows from those kicked back in office chairs sipping coffee. For that little stunt, I was told to never go on brigade frequency again. I also got to have a one-sided conversation with one of their Battalion staff officers later that night while I stood at attention in my dust caked body armor. He was sipping coffee.

The bottom line is that the helicopters needed to talk to someone who was actually on the ground in the fight. The leader back at the base wanted to be in charge because he had the title. Had he been there it would have been fine, but he was not, I was.

When you cannot be there, you need to have trained your leaders in such a way that you trust them to make the right decisions in a timely manner with the information they have.

There is a big difference between being there and being in charge. You may have a subordinate leader in charge somewhere out in the field. You do not have to be in charge of every little thing, but go see your people. Go "embrace the suck" with them for a while.

EMBRACE THE SUCK: Military mindset for loving the uncomfortable. Staying motivated and cracking jokes while being cold, wet, tired, and hungry is a great example of "embracing the suck."

This is not only true in a military environment. If you want your business to run well, be there. If you want your co-workers to take a topic seriously in a meeting, be there. I think of the television show "Undercover Boss." The Chief Executive Officer (CEO) of a company goes out in disguise and pretends to be a brand new employee. They go through training and talk with some of the people on the front line of their business to get the real scoop of how things are going. That is being there. Build a culture inside your company where all levels of leaders get down in the dirt with their people.

HOW TO MAKE IT A PRIORITY:

Being there is not as simple as it would seem. If you are out with your subordinates, you are not in the office and some things are not getting done. If you are not out in the field, you can do all the office work, but you will be violating Lesson 1. What do you do? Move out of your comfort zone, allow subordinate leaders to take charge and trust that some work can wait. My resident director, Jeff Korpi, at Northern Michigan University used an analogy of marbles and jars. You have 100 marbles to distribute in as many jars as you like. The jars have labels such as work, faith, family, fishing, etc. You can put a lot of marbles in your office jar, but then how many marbles are you putting into being out with your workers? If you put a lot of marbles in the out-and-about-jar, then you have to take some out of the being-in-the-office-jar. So how do you make being there a priority? Balance.

Push your subordinates to take care of the office business while you are out. Trust them to do what needs to be done. Give them some power by giving up some of yours. Each organization needs to figure it out on an individual basis, but keep in mind that great leaders are not usually remembered for the time spent in their office.

LESSON 1: SURROUND YOURSELF WITH SMART PEOPLE, THEN LISTEN TO THEM

I used to hear my dad say this all the time. He said that he was never smarter than anyone else. He simply surrounded himself with smart people, listened to them, then outworked them. This is a tough one for a lot of leaders. The leader is always supposed to know what to do, right? If you are leading a small team of people, it is pretty easy for you to be the smartest person in the group and know what to do all the time. When that group of people becomes larger, older, and more experienced, being the smartest person in the group becomes almost impossible. In classic Army fashion, they attempted to teach this lesson early in the life of a second lieutenant. The young lieutenant (LT) has basic skills, basic working knowledge of leadership, and zero experience. This young officer is then expected to lead a platoon of 20-50 Soldiers who have already proven their competency in their field.

If the platoon leader tries to be the expert on everything, they fail almost immediately. However, if the young officer takes advice from the folks that have been there longer, they will most likely be successful. As much as the Army places that young lieutenant in a position to fail, they set them up to succeed. As a platoon leader, the LT must answer directly to the commander. However, they are not alone. The army structures platoons with a leader and also a sergeant. Platoon sergeants are the most senior enlisted person in the platoon and are responsible for running the day to day operations following the intent and orders of the platoon leader. Platoon sergeants are "the smart people" and responsible for mentoring and training young lieutenants. LT's that listen to and accept mentorship from their platoon sergeants will be successful.

I did not even realize my own experience using this lesson until I was home from leading a Military Police (MP) company in Afghanistan. My Executive Officer (XO), Brice, had called me up for some Army chat. He had recently taken over a MP company and I enjoyed talking with him about his experiences and challenges. It was kind of my report card on developing him as a leader. I brought up the "surround yourself with smart people, then listen to them" idea. Brice started laughing. He said he could remember several times where most, if not all, of the senior leadership in the company were all on the same page except for me. He said I had a line, "OK. We will do it your way, but if it fails, we do it my way." I did not even realize I was doing it, but I was following my old man's advice. (My dad hates it when I call him old man.)

I have seen this play out as the "smart" person too. Sometimes I was listened to, and sometimes I was not. Try to remember a time when you were the smartest person in the room, and your opinion did not matter. How frustrating this can be!

After coming off of a full-time stint with the Army running the operations section of a 600 Soldier Battalion on a Monday through Friday basis, I was transferred to another organization. My boss's boss asked me to help update their shift change schedule. It was not originally my idea, but the way we had done it at the Battalion was simple, brilliant, and outside of the box. I pitched the plan to my boss's boss and he loved it. He brought in all of the other primary staff officers and I briefed them on the plan.

Most of them did not like it at first. The plan was not well liked at the Battalion at first either, but once I gave solid examples of ways this method improved the functioning of the staff and each section, some minds were beginning to shift. Here I was, a senior Captain, briefing much more senior officers. I was the smartest guy in the room, on that topic, and I was being listened to as well. What a great experience! I wrote up the plan and it was on its way to becoming the standard.

Two months later my boss's boss had been replaced and, without fully understanding the plan, the replacement scrapped it. When I saw we were back to the old way I went to talk with him about how and why the schedule was being replaced. I was told in a polite way that he did not have time for the opinion of a captain.

That is the best illustration I can give of first being trusted with a plan, then being told I was not important enough to have an opinion. Regardless of the new boss's intent, that was the message I received.

I see this lesson play out all the time in coaching. When attending coaching conferences, I will often sit in the front with a notebook, laser focused on the speaker and topic. They may not be the smartest person in the room, but they are the one willing to teach me.

The first session I attended at a Glazier Clinic was led by a very successful high school coach from Ohio talking about the Wing-T offense. Although I only intended to attend his 1-hour session, I ended up staying for three of his sessions and left with seven pages of notes. He was the smartest person in the room on the topic and I was thrilled to learn from him.

GLAZIER CLINIC: Glazier is an organization that hosts football coaching professional development all over the United States. Geared mostly toward high school teams, most clinics feature top college and NFL coaches.

A quick note about football coaches. On game day, we feel we have to have all the answers for every possible situation. When those young players look to us for a solution, we must have the perfect plan every time. At least that is how we sell it, if only on the outside. When it is not game day, a lot of us feel inadequate and underprepared. Most of us are sponges for information and are always looking for ways to improve our coaching and our team. I never want to be the smartest coach at a conference because then my opportunity to learn is less. My hope is that by attending the conference, I will be a little smarter than the coach on the other sideline come game day.

HOW TO MAKE IT A PRIORITY:

Push your subordinates to make decisions. Give them some constraints and some conditions to follow, then let them go! It is hard to give up the power, but at the same time, why did you hire them if not to be thinkers? If you hired them to be thinkers, why are you not letting them think? Once you properly set the conditions and constraints on your subordinates you might be amazed by what they can do. This lesson can best be remembered by the following: just because it is not the way you would do it, does not make it wrong.

Also, seek out mentorship from those who are smarter than you on a certain topic. I believe face-to-face mentorship is best, but in the world of videoconferencing and podcasts, it is not the only way to learn. Listen to podcasts on topics in which you are interested. Watch videos of speakers in a field you want to learn about. Reach out to someone with whom you are interested in talking. If you are not talking to them now or you email them and they say no, then you have lost nothing. If they say yes, you just found someone smarter than you. Listen to them.

"OK. We will do it your way. But if it fails, we do it my way."

LESSON 1: ASK THE STUPID QUESTION

This is a classic in the Army. Someone gets up to brief the room on a topic and says the acronym ILC 143 times in a 20 minute presentation. In the end, there are no questions, but no one knows what ILC means. I can guarantee that if you are in a group larger than five and you have a question, someone else has the same question, be the one to ask it. You may feel silly, but all of your peers will be thankful. Your presenter will look silly for thinking everyone knew what they were saying! We preach solid communication plans, then there is a stigma for trying to clarify the communication. Do not let this be you.

I had a boss in the Army, a two-star general, who was anti-acronym. During a briefing, he would ask, "What does XYZ mean?" A surprising amount of the time, no one in the room knew. He wanted clarity of communication. His thought process was to have less information that was better understood than more information with less understanding. This idea goes along with the difference between awareness and understanding. There is a lot of talk among leaders about situational awareness. There is a term that I think encapsulates this idea better: situational understanding, understanding the environment in which you are standing. You may be aware of the things going on around you, but do you understand the "why" or the "what" of them?

I had another boss, a Battalion commander, who was a very big believer in owning absolutely everything on your briefing slides. If you did, when the stupid question was asked, you could answer it. As long as it was not me, it was pretty funny when someone had an acronym on a slide they did not know. By learning to own every letter on my slides, I like to think I became very good at briefing in the Army. I was able to answer the stupid question before it was asked. The classic line at the end of each slide is "pending your questions...next slide." I would try very hard to walk the audience through a slide from the top left to the bottom right, answering any questions I thought they might have before I asked them if they had any. Usually, this worked out great. Once in a while there would be a stump-the-chump moment when someone in the audience would try to point out an error in my numbers or thinking. Since I had learned to own every number and letter on my slide, that did not work. If there was an issue, I had already brought it up and discussed how I planned to fix it.

STUMP THE CHUMP: When someone in the audience asks questions designed to trip up the presenter.

The stupid question is a daily occurrence in teaching. The difference is that it does not get asked. So, it is up to the teacher to ask the question. Something as simple as the statement, "The 19th amendment addressed women's suffrage," should to be followed up with the question "What is suffrage?" I am blown away at the amount of times a question is not asked, even though it is necessary to understand the material.

Another example comes from coaching. I am grooming some of the eighth graders I see every day in my classroom to play freshman football next year. I have placed them all in a Google Classroom and have been posting short videos teaching them various things about football. One item I covered was when the ball is run out of bounds, it is brought back to the nearest hash mark. This was something

I did not think I needed to cover, yet when players posted comments, that was the number one thing mentioned. Most of these kids had been playing football for two or three years and watching it for much longer, yet they had no idea the ball was always placed inside the hash marks. Do not take basic information for granted. Make sure the stupid question gets answered, even if you are the one who has to do the asking.

The bottom line is, ask the question nobody wants to ask. Ask the stupid question.

HOW TO MAKE IT A PRIORITY:

First off, never leave a meeting not knowing what was said. If information is shared, you are now responsible for it. (See Lesson 1: Own it!) Would you rather feel self conscious at the end of a meeting in which you learned brand new information but still asked the stupid question? Or would you rather feel silly a week later when you are asked about it again and did not know the answer? Put your pride in your pocket and ask the stupid question.

Second, flip the script and do not let people leave a meeting not knowing what you said. You can do this by watching the body language of your audience. The more you present, the better you will get at noticing the blank stare. Another way you can ensure your audience is comprehending what you are presenting is to back brief. There are many ways to do this, the simplest way is to ask open-ended questions and have your audience explain back to you what you just said. Depending on audience size, you may have them do this directly to you in three or four person groups or to another person. If you ask a stupid question, you are modeling to your subordinates that asking is not only acceptable but expected.

"Put your pride in your pocket and ask the stupid question."

LESSON 1:
FLIP THE PYRAMID
BE A SERVANT
LEADER

One way to think of a leadership model is as a pyramid. The leader is at the top, subordinate leaders are below, and workers are the base. Consider flipping the pyramid. The leader is at the bottom, supporting the subordinate leaders above them and the workers on top. This is very closely related to leveraging the talent around you.

You can think of being a leader in two ways: "I have to make myself successful," or "I have to make my subordinate leaders successful." If you concentrate on making your subordinate leaders successful, you will realize that you are working for them. On the organizational chart, they work for you. In practice, you work for them. By adopting this mindset, you will begin solving problems that matter. If your subordinate leaders are successful, you will be successful.

This is a balancing act when you are also a subordinate leader. You have to answer to your boss and your subordinates have to answer to you. If you make an active attempt to work hard for your subordinates, when the time comes, they will happily work to make you successful for your boss.

I tried very hard to live this lesson when I was a company commander in Afghanistan. I would make it a point to do whatever I could to help my platoon leaders be better leaders by working for them. Sometimes this involved hard conversations about things they were doing or failing to do. Sometimes I went to my boss with an issue I could not solve with my position or rank. Sometimes it involved going to other officers and realigning the chain of command.

Sometimes it was as simple as getting a piece of equipment or streamlining a process. Other times it involved something more complex. While in Afghanistan, we had to turn in all of the equipment we inherited when we got there. There were shipping containers full of items that had been acquired over the years. Since our unit was not going to be replaced, we were given the job of turning in all of the equipment. What a pain! There were a few times that my first sergeant, my XO and I had to arrange things for our subordinates to make them successful in this area.

My supply sergeant was great at his job, but needed to be in Bagram in order to conduct the equipment return. We figured out how to have him move up there from Kabul for weeks at a time to complete the necessary paperwork and handover of equipment as we sent it to him.

We figured out innovative ways to improve our communication plan with units conducting missions so we could get the radios that needed to be turned in up to Bagram. We did the same with the vehicles, encryption equipment, computers, and our company side-by-side. Some of these things seemed trivial, but they helped make other people's jobs easier and more efficient.

While working as part of the engineer battalion I had no subordinates, but because I worked for the battalion, I made it my job to be sure the companies could be successful. We would send out clear, concise mission orders in a timely manner. We streamlined the task assignment and reporting procedures so the units could spend less time on tasks for us and more time on being successful. It was a lot of work, but the way we saw it, us working for them meant the missions were getting completed faster and with great quality. There is a reason our motto was "Good as done!"

There is a running joke in the Army about officers doing things for their evaluation. When you see an officer doing something you may hear, "There's an Officer Evaluation Report (OER) bullet." If an officer is worried about their OER, they are not worried about their subordinates. If they are worried about making their subordinate leaders successful, their OER will take care of itself. None of the things I did were done so it would end up as a bullet point on my evaluation. Some things did end up on my evaluation, and some did not. The best evaluation I could hope for would be a superior saying, "If you want it done right, give it to VanDusen's unit."

Teaching might be the most concrete example of being a servant leader. I feel that my success is based solely on the success of my students. Think about how you define success. Is success based on standardized test scores, academic growth, or something that cannot be measured? I know I have been successful by the students who visit me long after they have left my classroom. The evaluation my principal has to complete on my teaching is important, but it will never compete with the 20 year old who walks back into my classroom to say how much they enjoyed learning how to learn.

I am on the Behavior Health Assessment Team at my school and its primary focus is on social emotional learning (SEL) or the soft skills that kids and adults learn such as grit, growth mindset, and social awareness. Five core competencies are further broken down into 29 areas. This is where the future (present?) lies in education. Making students successful in things such as emotional regulation, self-efficacy, and sense of belonging. I truly believe that if we can make students successful in SEL competencies, the test scores will take care of themselves.

Take care of your people by serving them and they will take care of you. This is not only true in evaluations, production, and grades but in being a human being. Stick to the basics.

HOW TO MAKE IT A PRIORITY:

To use a football analogy, are you working to be an all-state athlete or a state champion team? Each member of a team can either be an integral part that adds to the efficiency and productivity or they can merely take up space. Figure out new ways to make your team members successful. On a football team, it is the quarterback giving accolades to the offensive line during a press conference. In the Army, it is making sure all of your Soldiers sitting in defensive positions have hot coffee for breakfast. What does it look like for you? How do you make your teammates important?

"If your subordinate leaders are successful, you will be successful."

LESSON 1: MAKE A DECISION EVEN IF IT IS A BAD ONE

This one drives me absolutely insane! In the military, leaders are trained to make a decision. In the civilian world, not so much. People would rather form a committee, hold meetings, and not make a decision. If you do not make a decision, you cannot be wrong, right? I seems like many people are so scared to have their name associated with a bad decision that they would rather not make one at all.

I think leaders should get feedback, input, and ideas from their leaders. Then, the leader needs to make a decision. Here is the difference. If I form a committee and call three meetings over two weeks, hear opposing viewpoints or even take a vote, the people who were working hard on the opposing position are going to be upset and feel like they lost. They are still on the team and still have to help pull the rope in the same direction. On the other hand, if the leader assesses the facts and assumptions, solicits opinions from trusted advisors, and takes into account risk and reward, they can make and begin to execute a plan. The plan can be adjusted as more information becomes available, but taking the first step toward completion is the most important.

A lot of times I have only a vague idea of what to do, but I still take a step. It may not be in the right direction at first, but how will I know if I do not try? In a situation like this, I think of a compass. I am not sure where I am going, but if I take a step I have 180 degrees of possibly being right. Once that happens, things start falling in place or falling apart. Then you can zoom in to where you need to go and figure out how to get there. If you are stuck and stay where you are, tomorrow you will still be stuck. If you are stuck and try 10 things that do not work, you are still stuck, but you know to try something other than those 10 things. MAKE A DECISION!!! DO SOMETHING! ANYTHING! A failure is a try and a try is better than nothing.

When coaching a football game being prepared is a big part of the battle, but being able to adapt to what is happening on the field can be even bigger. Early in my coaching career, I would wait until halftime to make an adjustment on defense. If I was lucky, it would not be too late. As I would start to watch the film I would remember having feelings during the game that I should change something, but I would not make that decision until halftime. I started forcing myself to start making those gut feeling decisions at the quarter. This allowed me 12 minutes of seeing if my gut was right, most of the time it was. As I progressed through my career, I would trust my gut more and more and make decisions faster and faster, getting minor adjustments done in between each series. More often than not, my adjustments worked and by adjusting faster, we were much more dynamic and effective on defense.

Enter the world of me being an offensive play-caller. After coaching the defensive side of the ball for 14 years my head coach, Kevin Murdock, was retiring at the end of the season and wanted to groom me to take over. This put me back at square one when it came to coaching football. That year of calling offense with Kevin in my hip pocket was a great learning experience and forced me to make decisions quickly. Soon I would be on my own, but the lessons I learned under Coach Murdock would propel me faster into quality decision making than if I had not had that experience.

HOW TO MAKE IT A PRIORITY:

Challenge yourself to make a decision too fast. The larger the organization, the longer change takes from the top to the bottom or from the bottom to the top (see Lesson 1: Flip the pyramid. Be a servant leader). Sometimes decisions take a long time and require intense analysis of the possible outcomes. Take that time and make high-quality, analytical, decisions. Some decisions do not require that analysis. Challenge yourself to make smaller decisions faster. If you make a mistake because you made the decision too fast, then you will know your limits and you can slow down. That bad decision may also be a great learning tool for other things you have not yet thought about.

"If you're stuck and stay where you are, tomorrow you will still be stuck."

LESSON 1:
IF YOU HAVE TO TELL PEOPLE YOU ARE IN CHARGE, YOU ARE NOT

I love this one. "You will listen to me because I am the leader." No, you are not. You want to be, but you are not. When someone walks into a room, they should not have to ask, "Who is in charge here?" They should know. Are you really in charge or do you just hold the title of leader?

If you are the leader, you had better hope you are also in charge. Being a leader is not about a title or a name tag or a rank on your chest, it is about being in charge and making decisions. It is about coordinating people, places, and things to all mesh in a way that is efficient and makes sense. If you are that leader nobody will ask if you are in charge, they will know based on your actions, not your title.

We have all been in meetings where one person is supposedly in charge, but someone else is running the meeting. Maybe it is because they have knowledge of the topic or maybe it is because the person in charge really is not. The less prepared the leader is, the more this will happen. I remember sitting in a meeting for the Army and an open ended question was asked by the person in charge and the next 20 minutes was listening to two other Soldiers complaining and making excuses. The person that was supposed to be in charge never stopped it and never re-directed the conversation. He was not in charge at all.

Hopefully, you have also been in a situation where you walked into a room and immediately knew who was in charge. While attending a council meeting south of Baghdad in Al-Wahda, Iraq, there was no question who was in charge. There was a village elder we nicknamed Abe Lincoln (because of his beard) who was in charge, no question. He was not just in charge of that meeting, but of everything that happened in the area. He was a powerful man with whom I quickly formed a cordial relationship because I could tell that he was the man who made things happen. Although I never trusted him, I did respect his ability to get things done and we had a good working relationship while improving the security in his community. I do not think he had an official title, but he was definitely in charge. He did not have to tell me, he showed me.

Keep this lesson in mind for more than just the person who tells you they are in charge. If people have to tell you they are something, they probably are not. This is apparent on the sports field as well. Do you look good or are you good? I cannot stand a player who is cocky and arrogant, especially if they cannot back it up with their talent and hard work. Why are you pumping up the crowd? Why are you chirping at your opponent? Let the scoreboard do the talking. Do your work and the crowd will take care of itself. Work hard enough that you do not have the extra breath in your lungs to trash talk.

Are you a great leader, a great teacher, great at what you do? How do you know? Do you constantly have to go around telling others about how great you are or do they know you are great at your job for another reason? I know these may be hard questions to answer, but being a leader is hard work. Being in charge is hard work. Question yourself. Hopefully, you have some trusted colleagues you can ask as well. Go back to Lesson 1: Flip the Pyramid and see if you are working for the title on your desk or for the people who do not have their name on a desk. It can be scary to answer these questions honestly, but if you are truly looking to improve yourself and your organization, you will be bold in asking, humble in answering, and courageous in making it better.

One of my favorite quotes that illustrates this comes from Ralph Waldo Emerson, "Your actions speak so loudly, I can not hear what you're saying." Let your actions do the talking more than your words.

HOW TO MAKE IT A PRIORITY:

Forget your title, remember your job. What is your job and what does it look like to be successful? Do that. In the Army, it is easy because everyone wears their authority on their chest in the form of rank. A captain outranks a sergeant and a sergeant outranks a private. You are held accountable for your job based on your rank and position. The private world is a lot more fluid. Who is really in charge? If you have to tell people it is you, then it is not you.

"Forget your title, remember your job."

LESSON 1:
WRITTEN PLANS
WILL NOT GET READ

If you do it right, written plans can read like poetry and when followed, things work out pretty well. Most of the time. Well some of the time.

The Army has a format for giving missions called the Operations Order (OPORD) which can be amended by a Fragmentary Order (FRAGO). An OPORD is nearly all-inclusive complete with annexes, appendices to annexes, and tabs to appendices. Depending on the level of command, the complexity of the mission, and the personality of the commander, OPORDs can be very thorough and complete. They can also be vague. Bottom line: do not plan on anyone reading it, at least not all of it.

OPORD: A specific written format used by the Army for issuing tasks to subordinate units. Each OPORD contains five paragraphs: Situation, Mission, Execution, Sustainment, and Command and Control.

I wrote a ton of OPORDs and FRAGOs and I am guilty of not reading them. The main reason for not reading these directives in their entirety is that most people only care about what pertains to them. If I am in charge of securing a bridge for a convoy movement I will read everything pertaining to that part. The rest of it is not important to me.

The same thing happens in the civilian world. Think about it. If your phone vibrates and you see you have an email, do you read it? Maybe. If you see that it is longer than your elevator ride will you read it? Maybe not. There may be some important information in there, but it feels like a waste of time to read 85% of the stuff that does not pertain to you. As a leader, just assume it was not read. Want proof? Count how many times someone fails to do something and their supervisor says, "But I sent you an email..."

This leads to a very dangerous practice of tasking through text messages. You will read a text message, but it is no way to conduct business. So what do you do? As a leader, I believe it is important to chunk the information into sections that pertain to certain people. An OPORD does a really good job of this. Conduct an internet search for OPORD format

SMASH CONCEPT: Passing concept used to attack zone defenses. Placing the flat defender in conflict. The defensive line does not care, they just want to go get a sack on the quarterback.

or simply break things up into manageable chunks and make the headings bold.

I found the easiest way is to chunk information by project. This allows people to read about the project they are involved in and check out the other projects that may impact theirs or they are interested in. It also allows them to refer back to the document as the project moves further along. They may not have been interested in a certain aspect when it started, but as time goes on they may want to know more about a particular area.

I use this format in scouting reports for my football team. The defensive line cares very little how the opponent runs a smash concept to the outside flats. In turn, the free safety could care less that the left guard points his toes in the direction he is pulling, or holds his off hand differently on a pass set. With that in mind, I break up the report into different sections, so that different positions can read what is important to them. Some players will read the entire thing, some will read none of it. The players who do choose to read it are set up for success, they do not have to read the whole thing to get value.

Think about that email you got as you stepped into the elevator. If you see it chunked into sections, you will probably scroll to your section and read that part.

HOW TO MAKE IT A PRIORITY:

Once you realize long documents will not get read you need to find ways to make the information readable. Break things up, put them in smaller chunks. Get rid of the fluff and stick to the facts. Here is the kicker, if you are going to ask someone to read something, make sure they will use it later. None of us like busy work that is not useful, so get rid of it.

LESSON 1: SAND TABLES ARE AWESOME

In the Army, we sometimes use a sand table, which is a model of an objective. They can be elaborately built with mock buildings, cars, and roads or they can be three rocks with some lines drawn in the dirt. Sand tables give a visual representation of what is supposed to happen during the execution of a plan. It must have physical pieces that can be moved. I have seen digital sand tables, which are great for remote meetings, but they do not quite have the same effect.

So you can wrap your mind around what I am talking about, here are a couple of my favorite famous sand tables. In the movie "Con Air" when the convicts are planning to ambush the police, they use a sand table that involves beer cans and lines in the dirt. At one point one of the convicts points to a rock and asks, "What is that?" Someone answers, "That's a rock," and it gets tossed aside. In the movie "Back to the Future" Doc Brown makes a sand table of the path the DeLorean will take to get back to 1985. This is very elaborate, but Doc Brown makes a point to apologize that he did not have time to build it to scale or to paint it.

Sand tables provide a level of understanding that simply cannot be achieved with words and pictures. By physically moving items around the model, problems can become apparent that may not be identified otherwise. Problems can be solved and multiple scenarios can be acted out by moving items around on a sand table without moving things in real life.

Not sending a teenager back to 1985? You do not have a military application? That is fine! Sand tables can be used for anything. Using a sand table is simply another form of rehearsal for weddings, parades, professional development sessions, or potlucks. Try using a sand table and you might be surprised at how well it works and the shared understanding that is achieved.

There are two ways to walk through a sand table. The first way is probably the easiest to understand and execute. Walk through the entire operation chronologically. Start at the beginning and have the people responsible for moving the pieces in real life move the pieces on the sand table. Issues that individual planners did not see will quickly become apparent and be fixed before they become a crisis. Ensure that each planning group is taking notes, but also that there is an overall note-taker to identify friction points and areas where more analysis and planning is needed.

The second way to go through a sand table is by phase. Each planner states their specific tasks chronologically by phases. This can be a little more complex, but it will separate phases from each other so that issues in one area do not affect other areas.

Here is a basic example of how a sand table rehearsal might go for a simple meeting where a superior leader is receiving business information. This sand table could be as simple as a drawing on a whiteboard with magnets that are moved around representing each person or group.
The important part is to have people physically move something like a magnet, a sticky note or action figure.

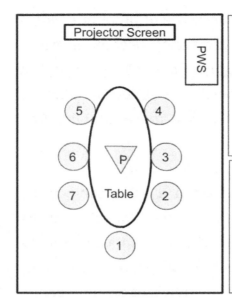

1- Leader Receiving the information
2- Logistics Manager
3- Financial Manager
4- Financial Assistant
5- Logistics Assistant
6- HR Manager
7- IT Manager

PWS: Presenter Work Station
P: Conference Phone

Upon initial set-up, the first change before the rehearsal even starts, is to place the assistants and the managers next to each other and to put the IT manager next to the PWS in case there are any technical issues.

Potential issues are already solved!

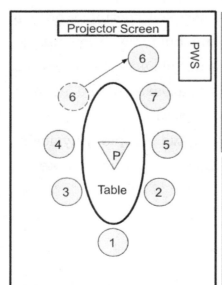

1- Leader Receiving the information
2- Logistics Manager
3- Financial Manager
4- Financial Assistant
5- Logistics Assistant
6- HR Manager
7- IT Manager

PWS: Presenter Work Station
P: Conference Phone

Manager and assistant distribution is now set up properly. The first person to present is the HR Manager (6). Therefore, the HR Manager moves to the front of the room near the PWS showing that he is presenting.

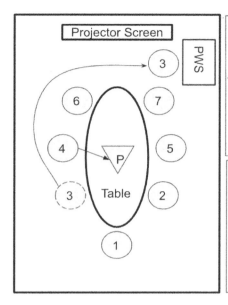

1- Leader Receiving the information
2- Logistics Manager
3- Financial Manager
4- Financial Assistant
5- Logistics Assistant
6- HR Manager
7- IT Manager

PWS: Presenter Work Station
P: Conference Phone

Next, the Financial Manager (3) moves to the PWS to present while the Financial Assistant (4) calls a person located remotely. Again, both physically move in order to show the process. For instance, if the Assistant doesn't have the phone number, they need to make sure they have it for the meeting.

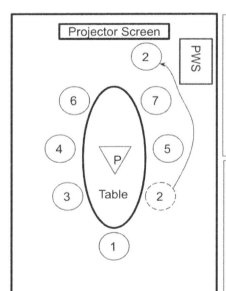

1- Leader Receiving the information
2- Logistics Manager
3- Financial Manager
4- Financial Assistant
5- Logistics Assistant
6- HR Manager
7- IT Manager

PWS: Presenter Work Station
P: Conference Phone

Finally, the Logistics Manager (2) projects a map on the screen and wants to use a marker to "connect the dots" for his boss. During the sand table rehearsal, he decides he wants to use red, green, and blue markers. He tells his assisstant to make sure they are present for the meeting.

HOW TO MAKE IT A PRIORITY:

Build one. You can make a sand table for workflow on a document through your company or to track your shopping trip through the grocery store. By moving pieces around a physical model, the understanding of everyone involved will skyrocket and you might discover issues you did not even know you had. Then, you can fix them before those issues become problems.

"By physically moving items around the model, problems can become apparent that may not be identified otherwise."

LESSON 1: REHEARSE EVERYTHING

Practice, rehearsal, walk-through, whatever you want to call it you have to do it. Think of a speech you had to give or a presentation at work. Did you rehearse it?

When I say rehearse everything, I mean everything. Will your computer time out? Do you require the internet? Can you connect to the Wi-Fi? (Pro Tip: Do not rely on the internet. Download it.) There are several types of rehearsals, from full blown everything-exactly-how-it-will-be rehearsals to in-your-head rehearsals and everything in between. (Remember the Lesson on the sand table?)

Even if you have never and will never run a qualification range for the Army, I am sure you will see some parallels in your planning process. I was the company commander for the 144 Military Police Company (Blackhats!). We had several ranges coming up where we would be honing our skills with our pistols, rifles, and machine guns. These ranges were not designed to familiarize ourselves with these weapons, but to increase our lethality and ability to operate all of our weapons during the day and night. I wanted each platoon to complete a range rehearsal at the armory. I had them set up a mini-range so they could walk through the procedures. Their platoon leader came and told me they were ready. My 1SG and I walked through the rehearsal as if we were shooters. When it was time to change out targets it was demonstrated that a sergeant would come behind the shooters and staple a new target up. I said, "Where's the stapler?" I was told, "It's in the range box." I said, "Go get it." With an eye roll, (I could not see it, but I am sure it happened) one of the non-commissioned officers (NCO) went to the box to retrieve the stapler. It was not there.

RANGE BOX: A literal box used to keep everything needed for a standard qualification range. White and red paddles to signal when the shooting line is ready, staplers, targets, scorecards, etc.

Turns out the stapler was borrowed from the range box and put in the sign-making kit. That simple part of the rehearsal put the stapler back in the range box (along with 5,000 staples). Had this not been done, the range would have been a madhouse trying to either find a stapler or find an alternate way of attaching targets. That extra five minutes at the armory saved who knows how much time at the range. Rehearse EVERYTHING.

Another story on rehearsals, this time from the football coaching realm. Our team was having a banquet for the football program and wanted to play a running slideshow during dinner. The initial plan was for a projector and screen to play the pictures for 30 minutes before dinner until the program was complete. When I went into the room to do the technology rehearsal, I spied the 42-inch TV that sits in the cafeteria. I knew that would be a lot better than the projector, but I did not have the correct cable to connect to the projector. It took me about 20 minutes to get it all figured out, including where I would plug in my laptop and have it sit while we were eating dinner. During the dinner planning process, I led a picture rehearsal with the parents who were in charge of the food. After the tables were set up I took a picture, then used my phone to draw a diagram of where everything would go: plates, hot dishes, cold dishes, desserts. I texted the pictures to the parents so when they showed up later with their athletes, spouses, younger children, and arms full of food and bags everyone knew exactly where to go. Without a picture rehearsal, the food situation could have gone sideways in a hurry. (See Lesson 1: Sand Tables are Awesome.)

HOW TO MAKE IT A PRIORITY:

Realize that it is hard to do things right the first time and there will be problems. To avoid that, rehearse it. If you are setting up a meeting with a projector and microphone, set it up ahead of time and make sure you know how all of the components work. If you need to dim lights at a meeting, know where the light switches are and how they work. If you need to introduce people and have them walk to the front of a room, take that walk. You can rehearse just about anything, and if it must be done right the first time, rehearse it.

LESSON 1: OWN IT

One of my biggest pet peeves is one not taking responsibility for one's actions. I see this all the time in the elementary setting. I presume it is a defense mechanism. If it is not my fault, I cannot get in trouble, right? When I have two students who disagree (He hit me! No, I didn't!) I take them in the hallway and we figure it out. Usually, their stories are exact opposites. The student who was accused of wrongdoing has a different definition of what happened. "I didn't hit. I tapped." "I didn't spit. I sighed." "I didn't shove. I pushed. That's not shoving!"

In the Army we always say the leader is responsible for everything the unit does or fails to do. I think the second part of that saying is important. Too often we see leaders who fail to take action, thinking that if they do not take action they cannot make a bad decision (see Lesson 1: Make a decision. Even if it is a bad one.) Be bold in your decision making, then own the result. If it is a good decision, great! If it is not, own that too. You just learned a lesson that someone who was too timid would never learn.

I was coaching a football game in Gladstone. Just before halftime, we went into our prevent defense. The only issue was that I was not able to get one of my players off the field. I told him that he was out for the next play. I had his replacement on the sideline with me, grabbing him by the back of the shoulder pads. As soon as the whistle blew I told him to "GO!" and he went, hollering out the name of the lineman he was replacing. The only problem was the player who was supposed to come off the field, did not. Gladstone went no-huddle and I was forced to call a timeout with just a few seconds left on the clock.

PREVENT DEFENSE: A defensive set usually used at the end of a half when your team is ahead is specifically designed to prevent a long touchdown pass.

If I had not called a timeout, we would have gotten a penalty, putting the other team within field goal range. Instead, the timeout prevented the penalty. It also stopped the clock. Because of this, I gave Gladstone 60 seconds to talk about how they were going to spend the remaining seconds of the half.

We held them, but I knew I had made a major coaching mistake that could have given the other team another score. In the locker room my head coach gave some adjustments on offense. Then, it was my turn. The first thing I did was admit my mistake and apologize. Everyone in Delta County knew what mistake had been made and who made it. I could have tiptoed around the idea that the linemen should have been faster or that Gladstone surprised us. I could have hidden from my mistake, but at what cost? I believe that by taking time to admit what I had done wrong and asking the team for forgiveness was worth its weight in gold. The team trusted me to take responsibility and own my decision. Because of that, they were given a model of how to own their behavior on the field. We made a few minor adjustments and held the other team to zero points in the second half.

Trust is a big issue in coaching. I like to believe the fact that I owned up to my mistake right away made the players trust me. They knew I made mistakes, but also knew I coached hard to win. We all make mistakes. When they happen are you going to deflect responsibility or own it?

HOW TO MAKE IT A PRIORITY:

This will never happen inside of your organization if the leadership does not model it. The easiest way to own it is to admit and, if applicable, ask forgiveness for your mistakes. It is hard to be mad at someone if they have already admitted to being wrong about it. The inverse is true. If you make a mistake and refuse to own it and the consequences, you will very quickly turn your team against you and ownership will not happen in that organization. If you want others to own their mistakes, own yours first.

"The first thing I did was admit my mistake and apologize."

LESSON 1: HAVE A PLAN FOR ABSOLUTELY EVERYTHING

This is an impossible task, but you have to think about it. When you are leading an organization, you have to assume things will go wrong. You have to think ahead and prevent problems, if possible. You will not be able to prevent them all, but you will be able to prevent some. For the problems you cannot prevent or the problems you may not foresee, you must have a plan in place to deal with them.

My Military Police company training took place in Florida before our deployment to Afghanistan. This trip was a complete disaster. The transport of people and equipment from Michigan to Florida and Florida to Michigan was flawless (thanks Brice and Sean). Other than that, we had one problem after another in Florida: delays, mishaps, and massive leadership challenges. We were very reactive, instead of proactive, in dealing with issues and were constantly fighting to get ahead on our planning cycle. I had a problem I could not predict but was forced to deal with it.

MILITARY POLICE: The 144 MP Company had approximately 120 MP Soldiers and 30 support staff (supply, administration, etc.) that were trained in mobility support (armed security for convoys), area security (providing armed security to stationary assets and responding to attacks), law and order (law enforcement for military members and training host nation police forces), internment/resettlement operations (operating military prisons and enemy combatant facilities), and police intelligence operations (investigation techniques).

We were already late for a training event and I had a whole company of Soldiers get stuck in a bus on a back road. Not just stuck, but call-a-wrecker-and-wait-two-hours stuck. As I stood on the far side of the stuck bus with my platoon leaders around me, I realized they were all looking to me for answers and I should probably think of something.

We came up with the idea of moving the back part of the company that was not stuck, around the long way. Even though they would be late to training, they would at least get there. At the same time, we sent a deuce-and-a-half full of troops back to the main road where they would wait for the bus that was dropping off the first load of Soldiers. The bus and the deuce-and-a-half would continue ferrying Soldiers until they were all at the training site. I left my senior mechanic and her team to deal with the bus and incoming wrecker. I put a platoon leader in charge of the first bus of Soldiers and got them to training. I would ride with the second wave of Soldiers to the training with my first sergeant, ensuring everyone made it from the staging point to the training site.

DEUCE-AND-A-HALF: Slang for the Army 6x6 cargo truck used to transport Soldiers and equipment. A rougher ride you will never find as in the back of a deuce-and-a-half!

The next problem was getting Soldiers from the training site back to the barracks. That was an unforeseen problem as well. However, we had some time to deal with making sure Soldiers had a ride back to the barracks and time for their dinner as soon as training was over.

Even more fluid than an Army exercise, is teaching in an elementary school. There were a few times I did not have a plan for something until it happened. I always had a plan for the basics like a fire drill, lockdown drill, or child who starts screaming. I did not have a plan for the things I did not think would happen, or was too naive to think it would happen.

Let me pose a question: What would your plan be if a young student came to you and said there was mud on the floor and another student had stepped in it? Now, what would you do if it was not mud? I did not have a plan for a first grader pooping their pants in my room. I should have, other teachers had it happen in their classrooms. So, I did the best I could.

After that issue was resolved, I strategically placed paper towel rolls, garbage bags, and towels around my room. That specific incident did not happen again, but I did end up with some puddles on the floor when it was not raining. Because of my previous experience, I had a plan in place ready to spring into action.

Sometimes having a plan for absolutely everything means coming up with a plan on the spot. Cool heads and common sense will prevail. No pressure, though every eye is on you.

HOW TO MAKE IT A PRIORITY:

Make a game plan. Rehearse. Try to sabotage your own plan so you can critically think of solutions before those situations become a crisis. This can quickly go to the extreme, but there are several things you can identify during rehearsal for which you can have a contingency plan.

By thinking of these alternate ways of accomplishing the same task, you will not only be prepared for the current mission, but you will instinctively become better at devising plans and thinking outside the box. Thus, when the school bus full of Soldiers gets stuck, you will already be practiced in making a plan for the unplanned.

"Try to sabotage your own plan so you can critically think of solutions before those situations become a crisis."

LESSON 1: IF IT IS IMPORTANT GET A TEACHER IN FRONT OF THE GROUP

At about my 17-year mark in the Army, online training was very popular. I really cannot stand online training. I got upset when I was told I needed to attend an important online training I was missing. It was then I started saying, "If it was that important, someone would stand in front of me and teach it to me." I like to think that most people would agree with me. I see online training as a way to get leaders out of leading and teachers out of teaching.

What happens when you are in an online training? Don't lie. You leave the training window open while doing other work and check back every few minutes to click to the next page. When you get to a learning review or quiz you use your impressive test-taking skills and get just enough correct answers to pass.

People screenshot quizzes or take pictures with their phones, they share answers. No real learning takes place, you simply get through the class, print the certificate, and your organization can say you are trained. It is not important enough for someone to present the material to you in a way that is meaningful so you will actually know what the heck you are doing.

This goes beyond the material. It is about relationships with other students and the instructor. When it comes to learning as an adult, there are very few of us that cannot apply personal experiences to teaching. The Death by Power-Point method of teaching should never happen. It is disrespectful to the students. There are methods for breaking up large groups so they can learn the material as well as teach each other.

DEATH BY POWER–POINT: When a presenter projects a powerpoint slide deck with too many slides, too many words on each slide, and insists on reading it to you.

With all the madness that was 2020, online everything has been thrust from the fringes to the mainstream. I still maintain the position that in order for learning to take place, a teacher needs to be present. The teacher may be on a computer screen, but they are still there. This is where relationships really make a difference. I had the ability to be face-to-face with my 8th graders for a good percentage of the time that fall. When we were forced to go online, we had already established our relationship and how the class operated. Honestly, it was probably more of a hiccup for me than the students. They did not skip a beat.

On the flip side, in my Army teaching job, I have never met my students that fall in person, and probably never will. They attend the online class one weekend a month from all over the country and we all leave our cameras off to preserve bandwidth. Granted, all of my students are 30 to 40 year old adults who want to be there, but the relationships are not the same. In my 20 plus years in the Army I can tell you about all kinds of exciting training events, but I can tell you a lot more about the people I was with in the trainings.

Anyone who has taught a group of kids or adults can assess their level of engagement by reading their faces and body language. I have been told by several people that I cannot hide my expression. I have had teachers ask what I was thinking without saying a word or raising my hand. This is much more difficult to do during online classes. Even when the cameras are on it is very hard to read the expression on a person's face in their little picture on the screen.

Another interesting thing that happens when students are in a room together is the side conversation. Students young and old usually try to keep those conversations secret, but they never are. Some instructors get upset at the side conversation because the focus is taken off of them. I view side conversations as an extension of learning. If someone heard or saw something that formulated an idea strong enough that they felt the need to share right away, then it might just be worth listening to.

There is a lot of instructor skill in drawing that out without sounding like a jerk. "Hey, John! Do you want to share what you and Sally were just talking about?" To me, this sounds like a 1988 first grade teacher. A skilled instructor can draw the side conversation out and enrich the main conversation with something like "I feel like what we were talking about has really made some of you think. Take 60 seconds to share your thoughts with your partner." Then while they are sharing, quietly ask them to share with the group. It works wonderfully and brings those side conversations into the light. That does not happen during online training, even when a class is live.

In some ways, the online format works out better for my Army students. Nobody is traveling on a Friday night after work, or on a Sunday night after class. Everyone has the luxury of being in their home with their family at night, something the Army frequently takes away. However, when we joined the Army, we knew we would be taken away for different things and we signed up anyway. Although I feel very blessed that I do not have to do the driving, and I love spending time with my wife on the Saturday evening of my Army weekend, I still feel cheated somehow. The training we are doing is important. We do have an instructor in the front of the room, but it is not the same to me.

HOW TO MAKE IT A PRIORITY:

What is important? Prioritize the training needs and requirements of your organization. If it is important, figure out how to put a teacher out in front. If it is not important enough to utilize a teacher, why are you doing it? The second part of this lesson is giving quality education. You can teach until you are blue in the face, but if your students do not learn anything, everyone is wasting their time. In general, the more your students talk to each other, the more they will learn. Have them talk with their shoulder partner, in small groups, mixing with other groups. The key to engaging lessons is engagement. Keep your students engaged.

"I see online training as a way to get leaders out of leading, and teachers out of teaching."

LESSON 1: IT IS NEVER TOO LATE TO DO THE RIGHT THING

There are two ways to do the wrong thing. The first way is doing the wrong thing because you do not know you are doing it wrong. This happens often. I have to believe most of us do not wake up in the morning and say "MAN! I just want to jack some stuff up today!"

I had been coaching offensive linemen at junior high and varsity levels for about five years when I realized I was using the chutes wrong. The chutes are a contraption of bars that make five small tunnels for offensive linemen to take their first steps in to ensure they are keeping a low center of gravity and low body position. Because they are made out of pipes, if someone's body position is too high, it tickles the top of their helmet.

I always lined the players up in the cutout of the chute to get ready for their turn. I forget exactly how I figured it out, but I realized those cutouts were for players holding blocking bags. GENIUS! Why didn't I think of that?

That day I jogged my linemen over to the chutes and they lined up like they always have. I showed them the right way and everyone had a lightbulb moment. I was not doing it wrong on purpose, I was a victim of my own ignorance. I was doing it the wrong way because I did not know it was wrong. It was not too late to change course and do the right thing, I fixed it.

Another example comes from my first year of teaching. In my eighth grade math class, I made a number line on the floor. I thought I was brilliant in that I would have students stand on the number line and we would add and subtract positive and negative integers. They could move themselves along the number line and really see what was happening.

It was great for most of my students, but I had a few in desks on the other side of the room who always saw the number line in reverse. To them I was actually making it more confusing. I did not know I was doing it wrong until I listened to some of their reasoning after a quiz. I had three or four students give the same backwards reasoning and I knew I had messed up. The next morning that number line came up off the floor and went on the wall. It was not too late to change course and do the right thing, I fixed it.

You can even trace this Lesson back to the Bible with the Apostle Paul. He used to find, persecute, and kill Christians. It took God striking him blind for him to understand he was doing the wrong thing because he did not know it was wrong. He changed course and did the right thing, he fixed it.

The second way to do the wrong thing is when you know it is wrong. There are many right reasons to do the wrong thing. Read that again.

While deployed to Iraq and Afghanistan some of the things I did could be considered, by some, to be the wrong thing. However, if it came down to the safety of my Soldiers, I would always do what was in their best interest. Always. I do not think anyone can deny they have done the wrong thing on purpose because it was warranted.

Disclaimer: I never did anything illegal. I never broke the law. I would never condone law breaking behavior or tolerate it from myself, my subordinates, or my superiors.

If you are doing the wrong thing, and you know it is wrong, that is when you need to take a look at yourself. There is a fine line here where you can trick yourself into justifying your actions. Life is hard and sometimes we do things we are not proud of.

There was a short time in my life when I was drinking a case of beer every other night if not every night. Long story short, I was just back from Afghanistan and my wife at the time was in the process of leaving me. I sat in my basement and drank beer. That was my coping mechanism. I knew it was wrong, but I did it anyway.

Again, we can use the Apostle Paul as an example when he explained how he is in a constant struggle with sin in Romans 7:19, "For I do not do the good I want, but the evil I do not want is what I keep on doing."

After several weeks, I got over myself and started doing the right thing. I started to fill the void in my life with good people. I joined the volunteer fire department and was active in the American Legion. Probably the best thing that could ever have happened to me was joining a men's group at church. I had another fall soon after, but eventually, I squared myself away. I changed course and did the right thing, I fixed it.

SQUARED AWAY: Used in the Army to complement a Soldier on performing at an above average level.

HOW TO MAKE IT A PRIORITY:

First you have to be true to yourself and identify your values. What is important to you? Be honest. No one can answer this question for you. At the top of my list is faith and family. You have to decide what is at the top of your list. Have people around that will hold you accountable. Build healthy relationships. You can find those people in a lot of places such as work, church, and other professional organizations. The hard part is that it is much easier to find unhealthy relationships with people who will not hold you accountable. Be careful with which group you associate.

LESSON 1: YOU PLAY HOW YOU PRACTICE

Most of us have heard it said that you need to practice how you play. This is true, but hard to wrap your brain around. The truth is you will play exactly how you practiced.

It does not matter what the game is, you cannot just "turn it on" at game time. If you stop blocking before the whistle in football practice, you will stop blocking in a game. If you walk up the court during basketball practice, you will walk during a game. If you ease up in practice, you will ease up in a game.

A perfect example of this comes from my little league playing days. When we lived in Moore, Idaho, (population 183) there were only a few other kids to play with that were my age. In the spring after school and all summer long we would go to the local park and "practice pitching." This also involved practicing catching, hitting, backflips off the swing, going to the little candy store to buy baseball cards and checking for the "jackpot" in the newest Beckett magazine. My friends and I would basically leave our house after morning chores and return as the street lights came on, usually with a break somewhere in the middle for a peanut butter sandwich or a bowl of cereal. No cell phone. No social media. No worries.

When we were batting, the hitter would stand at the edge of the small, semi-enclosed area that housed two picnic tables while the pitcher stood in the middle of the park. If a pitch got past you, it would inevitably end up bouncing around the enclosure forcing us to put down our bat and crawl under a table to retrieve it. The easiest and fastest solution was to simply reach out and catch an inside pitch and toss it back to the pitcher. We did this all the time.

As a result of our consistent practicing, my friends and I always did fairly well in all-star tournaments out of town. It was at one of these all-star games that I played exactly how I practiced. It was a game under the lights that made us all feel like professional baseball players. I was up to bat and here came an inside pitch. What did I do? Obviously, I reached out and caught it. The look of panic on my face as I snapped my head back to the umpire was met by his look of astonishment. I dropped the ball straight to the dirt and stood there, not sure what was going to happen next. The umpire took off his mask and said, "I'm not sure if you should take your base or be out." Silence, then, "Take your base."

I had played exactly how I had practiced and did exactly what I knew how to do. I was able to advance to first base, but I could just as easily have been called out.

I do not know if it is true, but I have heard a story that comes out of Iraq in 2003. A squad gets ambushed and returns fire. When it is time to move, the sergeant has to yell at a private because he is bent over picking up his brass casings. Picking up his brass! Does this kid not know he is in a gunfight?

BRASS: The component of ammunition that contains the primer and powder. When the projectile exits the barrel on its way to the target, the brass is ejected onto the ground. It is not made of brass, but it has a brass color. After training events, all units must pick up all the brass they can find and turn it in the ammunition supply point.

Yes, of course he does. He also knows, based on previous training ambushes, he would have to pick up his brass and turn it in. He learned that if he can pick up a bunch of it right away, he will not have to be picking up brass when he could be sitting on his bunk playing a video game.

The last 50 practice gunfights the private had been in, he took a few seconds to pick up his brass. Now that he was in a real gun battle, he did exactly as he had trained. He was playing exactly how he practiced. It seems simple and silly, but in a high-stress situation, you will play exactly how you practice.

As I write this, I will be entering my 13th year of coaching. I learned something this fall that was so simple, yet so profound. The JV Head Coach, Kevin Murdock, had the team running sprints at the end of practice for conditioning. After the third one, he said, "Extra point team! You have to make this one, it's tied at 20." The team, starting to get tired, jogged over to the 3-yard line and kicked the extra point. Then, they went back to the sideline for sprints. Three sprints later he said, "Punt team! We have to get it out of our end zone!" Breathing heavily, they jogged over to the 5-yard line and punted the ball out of our end zone, then went back to the sideline. After three more sprints Kevin said, "Two-point conversion!" The team lined up, executed the play, then practice was over.

It was a simple thing to do, but it played out just that way for our last game of the season. With the score tied at 20 with a conference rival, our JV team drove down the field and scored. With one minute and 43 seconds left in the fourth quarter, sore legs and out of breath, they also punched in the two-point conversion. The JV team won that game 28-20 and clinched the conference title. They played exactly how they had practiced.

Think of ways to make your practice more like a game and you will be better off.

HOW TO MAKE IT A PRIORITY:

This can be really easy, or really hard, based on the culture of your organization. Sometimes failing at something is the best motivator for doing it right. Unfortunately, failing when it counts can be downright painful. How do you prevent this? When you are training, make it as real as possible. Make it harder than it will be when you do it for real. If you are training to give a sales pitch, give it to your team and tell them to ask you the hard questions. Tell them to find different ways to sabotage your presentation. If you can manage the rough seas people close to the project will cause, you will be well prepared for the smooth sailing of presenting in front of laymen.

LESSON 1: A HANDSHAKE IS WORTH A THOUSAND EMAILS

My favorite phrase as a leader: "I sent you an email." Maybe you did, but I do not care because the task is not done and it needs to be.

While I was working full time for the 107 Engineer Battalion out of Ishpeming, Michigan (Michigan Army National Guard), in the first 120 days of 2016 I was home 61 days and went to training events 59 of those days. I got really good at traveling and I loved it. The biggest issue during that time was attempting to coordinate a Joint Readiness Training Center (JRTC) rotation at Fort Polk, Louisiana with a higher headquarters out of South Carolina (I love the 218 MEB), and a higher-higher headquarters out of Indiana. It would have been fine if we were participating in a combat training rotation, but we were doing a domestic response rotation.

DOMESTIC RESPONSE: When National Guard and Army Reserve units assist within the United States. Our mission was to provide support for local municipalities in the event of a Chemical, Biological, Radiological, Nuclear, and high yield Explosives (CBRN-E) occurrence that they could not handle on their own.

It was painfully clear the JRTC is very good at training folks to go to war, but not well versed in teaching domestic response. There is a huge difference and it caused me to have to travel to Fort Polk three times within 30 days.

JRTC: Some of the best combat training in the world happens at Fort Polk, LA. Units are able to train in near-combat conditions against a well trained and regulated opposing force consisting of other Soldiers as well as role players acting as villagers, terrorists, and diplomats. If you will see it in combat, you can train on it at JRTC. The National Training Center in Fort Irwin, CA provides similar, realistic training events for units preparing to deploy.

I had a small team working with me who made several phone calls and sent countless emails, but at the end of the day, we were only able to iron out our issues when sitting across the desk from the person who was supposed to be helping us.

Equipment from all different kinds of military units was constantly moving on and off of Fort Polk via truck and rail. Coordinating all of that movement to ensure it was streamlined and on time was the responsibility of the Fort Polk travel office. As we were standing in the travel office at Fort Polk, a travel representative said to me, "You need to have your travel office call me immediately." I looked at him with a quizzical look and pointed to Sergeant First Class, Ben Proehl, who was standing by my side and said, "That's him. He coordinates all of our personnel and equipment movement." The rep gave me an equally quizzical look and said, "It can't be!" I got a stern look on my face and said, "It most certainly is...." As it turns out, Ben had everything they needed. I believe the team in Fort Polk worked with one National Guard unit per year, so it was understandable that we did not communicate well with each other. We were both at fault due to the distance.

It was a simple thing, but without physically looking someone in the eye, sometimes complex issues will just never be understood by all parties involved. It is much harder to tell someone no when they are standing at your desk.

The heavyweight boxer, Mike Tyson, once said, "Everyone has a plan until they get punched in the face." No one is at risk of that while being a keyboard warrior. To find proof of this, you have to look no further than your Twitter feed. The things said on social media would never be said in a face-to-face conversation. People feel safe behind their keyboards. They are safe from having to deal with the real consequences of their words. Please note that I am not advocating punching anyone in the face, deserving or otherwise.

What I am saying is that before you hammer someone on Facebook or in an email, ask yourself if you would be willing to say the same thing if you were standing together in an elevator. That may change the perspective and the tone of your response.

HOW TO MAKE IT A PRIORITY:
If it is important, complex, or easily misunderstood, it probably needs to be done in person. I see communication as a spectrum with text-based messages being the easiest to send and track, but also the easiest to misunderstand, to sitting at a

table looking the other person in the eye. It is the hardest to do, depending on physical distance, but it is the easiest to ensure situational understanding. Video chat services like Google Hangouts and Zoom are fantastic tools and can help bridge the gap between a phone call and a plane ticket. If you opt for the plane ticket, let me know. I will give you the hottest info on where to eat and get coffee at O'Hare.

LESSON 1: TAKE CARE OF YOURSELF

On December 5, 2009 the Florida Gators led by Coach Urban Meyer took on Coach Nick Saben's Alabama Crimson Tide at the Southeastern Conference (SEC) football championship in the Georgia Dome. Football fans will recognize some of the players in that game such as Tim Tebow and Mark Ingram.

With a minute and eighteen seconds left in the first half, Florida kicked a 32 yard field goal to bring the Gators within a touchdown of Alabama with a score of 19-13. That was the last score of the night for the team from Gainesville as the Tide rolled to a 32-13 victory.

On December 6, at 4:30 a.m. Coach Meyer was rushed to the hospital with chest pains and a tingling sensation on his side. In his book, Above the Line, Urban Meyer outlines those events and talks about placing his work above his well being and how it literally put him in the hospital. He also talks about making his self care a priority. After a small break in coaching, Urban Meyer went on to Ohio State to coach the Buckeyes for seven seasons, posting a record of 54 wins and only 4 losses. (See Lesson 1: It is never too late to do the right thing.)

You do not have to be a top division one college football head coach for this to happen. You can do it leading your own household! We hear "Take care of yourself," all the time. What does that mean? It can mean different things to different people, but I think the big three are diet, exercise, and sleep. Diet affects so much about us. I am not a dietitian like my wife, but I know the best way to improve your diet is to eat more vegetables, drink more water, and eat less sugar.

I drive a lot for the Army. When it is a weekend I have Army training, I jump in my truck after work on a Friday and head for the Armory. Sometimes after work on a Friday means I leave at 3:30 and sometimes, if we had a football game that night, it means I leave at 10:30. At one point in my Army career, I was driving a little over 500 miles one way for drill. Looking back, that was crazy! Now I drive a little over 200 miles, which can still be horrendous, but a lot more manageable. I also drive a lot to be with my son. He lives about 90 miles away, but is with me on most weekends, holidays, and school breaks. Sometimes I will drive up after work to watch him play baseball or basketball, then drive home right after. Those miles are well worth it, yet hard on my self care. During all that driving, the worst stop is the gas station. Coffee? Yes, please, extra cream! King Size Snickers? Absolutely! I drink coffee to stay awake on the road, I eat the candy bar because I talk myself into thinking it is a good idea. I am getting better. I drink my coffee with less vanilla creamer and I pick out healthier snacks, but I really need to think about it. Specifically, I need to think about what I will feel like the next day.

At school this is tough. There are always students moving about with cupcakes and cookies for their birthday. Every holiday is filled with goodies and every staff meeting is accompanied by pop and treats. I have to stay completely away. I cannot even walk in the teacher lounge when I know there is a box of doughnuts in there. I do not have a good answer for maintaining will power in these situations because I have none. I use the do-not-go-within-30-feet method. Sometimes it works, sometimes not.

Look at your habits at work and at home. In the course of your routines, are you tempting yourself by walking past the goodie table all the time? Maybe a change in habit is called for, change the bathroom you use at work so it does not take you past the pop machine. You may have to get downright aggressive about changing your habits, or your habits will most certainly change you.

Exercise is a classic "talk myself out of it" thing, especially when traveling. However, I always feel so much better when I take the time to get on the treadmill. Take the advice of Nike, "Just do it!" You will feel better and if you feel better, you are better. If you are better, you will lead better. I have found that if I get up in the morning and go workout, it sets my entire day up for success. On the flip side, if I try to justify to myself that I will workout after work, it rarely happens. Now that it is a habit, when my alarm goes off at 4:00 in the morning, I get up fairly easily. I get my coffee and my book and read until it is time to go to the gym at 5:00.

Not only has this helped my physical body, but my mental self as well. Starting the day off with something worthwhile or interesting to get my brain moving, then getting my body moving, is a recipe for a successful day. This goes hand in hand with diet. Am I springing out of bed because what I ate yesterday energized and nourished my body? Or am

I sluggish getting out of bed because the pizza grease and growler of beer is still sloshing around and my body is working to break it down and get it out?

Sleep. Ouch. I should not even be talking about this. Since the spring of 2007, I can count on one hand how many good nights of sleep I have gotten. I am not good at it. I know I feel better, but I just cannot turn my brain off. When I lay down my body will rest, but my brain will not.

Unfortunately, the only way I can get sleep is by using medicine prescribed to me by my doctor. It is not ideal, but it does work. I rarely feel rested. I have seen several specialists on this because I believe sleep is very important. While you are asleep, your physical body has time to repair itself. Also, your mind is able to sort through all of the stimuli throughout the day and make sense of it all.

While I was a resident advisor (RA) in college, I started taking 12 minute naps. My RA job would sometimes keep me up until 2:00 or 3:00 in the morning and I also liked duck hunting which required me to be up at 3:30 or 4:00 in the morning. Sometimes I was pretty tired when I hit the marsh. When I would get home and clean up, I would try to squeeze in a 12 minute nap. I do not remember where I got the number 12, but it seems to work. I take a stocking cap and pull it down low over my eyes to block out the light and keep my head warm. I lay on my bed and try to relax as many muscles as I can. I never really fall asleep, but a lot of times that 12 minutes will be just the rest I need to carry on with the rest of the day. I think of it like quickly charging your cell phone. I do not do this as often now, but it is still in my toolbox.

HOW TO MAKE IT A PRIORITY:

You need to schedule self care exactly how you schedule everything else. If you look at your calendar and see meetings, conference calls, and a list of things you must get done, you should also see time at the gym, food prep, bedtime, and time for your family and faith. If you pack your day full of meetings, tasks and activities you will not do anything that you do not plan. So, plan it. That is the only way you will make time for it. List your priorities in a hierarchical way and make sure you and your family are on the top of the list. Three things will always be on the top of my list: Jesus, my wife, and my son. Those three will always be above work, coaching, the Army, house, car, etc. To make them a priority, I also have to make myself a priority.

LESSON 1: TELL YOUR SUBORDINATES HOW THEY ARE DOING

As I am writing this sentence, I am 11 days shy of being in the Army for 18 years. In those 18 years, I have received many evaluations. Some were very well written and provided an accurate snapshot of my performance. Others were very generic with broad comments that could have been written about almost anyone. Guess which ones the great leaders wrote. In the Army, leaders are supposed to counsel their subordinates at least quarterly. This is supposed to be on paper and reviewed at the next quarterly counseling session. At the time I write this book, I have been counseled on paper exactly zero times. This absence of counsel is not fair to the people who work for you, not just in the Army, but in every leadership position.

To some people, the word counseling has a stigma of negativity. However, if used properly, it can be very successful. A good counseling session has a few main parts: purpose, key points, plan of action, leader responsibilities, and assessment. In full disclosure, these parts are from the Department of the Army Form 4856 Developmental Counseling, however it is a great format for any organization.

Purpose: Why are you sitting down today? It could be a quarterly meeting to see how things are going. It could be an event, good or bad, that you want to make sure is documented. For instance, if an employee has a chronically messy desk, what a great use of a developmental counseling form. On the flip side, if you have an employee who runs a conference and does a job that is above and beyond their pay grade, what a great use of a developmental counseling form. This form can also be used if someone is going to a training event or conference to lay out your expectations and theirs.

Key Points: This is the bread and butter of the counseling session. If it is event-oriented counseling, this can be pretty brief. Personally, I like to have conversation starters listed and let that guide our session. Keep notes and paint a picture of their performance.

Plan of Action: In this section you can talk about the future. What do they want to accomplish? What training do they want? This will help you help your subordinates when it comes to their advancement.

Leader Responsibilities: This is where you identify the things you need to do, as the leader, to make your subordinates successful in their plan of action. When you write down, in front of your subordinate, what you are willing to do to help make them successful you keep yourself accountable to your workers.

Assessment: This is the most important part, and the most underutilized. Once a counseling session has taken place, the notes need to find their way to the next session. The first thing that should be covered in the subsequent counseling sessions, is the assessment of the action plan and leadership responsibilities. What did they do as a leader? How did they do it? Did they achieve their goals? Were their goals too easy or too hard? What a great tool to start meaningful conversations about the workplace!

HOW TO MAKE IT A PRIORITY:

Schedule time to evaluate your subordinates during the most productive part of your day. If you make it an afterthought, it will be an afterthought and will be left behind. You owe it to your subordinates to tell them how they are doing. Not just for you, not even just for them, but for your organization. Your job is to make your organization runs as efficiently as possible and you cannot do that if your people do not know how they are doing.

LESSON 1: BE YOURSELF

In the movie "Necessary Roughness," the head coach gets hospitalized and the assistant coach has to take over. The assistant, who is usually in a cut off sweatshirt, sweatpants, and hoodies, puts on a tie and a sports jacket trying to emulate the head coach. It does not work. At half-time, he rips off the shirt and tie, throws the whistle, and goes into a tirade of football and profanity that motivates his players. It works...for him. He was not a tie and whistle guy, he was a t-shirt and yell type of coach. He tried to be like the head coach in order to be a head coach. This does not work. Be yourself.

Before you can be yourself, you have to know yourself. Ask yourself: Who am I? You might be surprised at how hard it is to answer this question. Remember, there are things you do that are not who you are. It might help to go back to the circular room with four sides. The things you do are the sides, but who you are is the person walking around the room.

In the book The Art of War by Sun Tzu, the author stressed the importance of knowing who you are. He said, "Know the enemy and know yourself; in a hundred battles you will never be in peril. When you are ignorant of the enemy, but know yourself, your chances of winning or losing are equal. If ignorant both of your enemy and yourself, you are certain in every battle to be in peril."

That does not mean you have to be good at everything. It means you have to know what you are good at and what you are not. In many of his lessons, Sun Tzu stresses the importance of knowing your strength and magnifying it while shrinking your weakness. He combines that with the idea of attacking the enemy where they are weak and avoiding their strengths.

Before you can magnify your strengths and minimize your weaknesses, you first have to know what they are. When you are not in a leadership role, it is easy to say what you would have done in certain situations and criticize the leader in charge. Instead of criticizing, try to understand the decision based on the leader and their long term vision. Maybe they do not have a vision or maybe it is something you cannot or will not see right away. Maybe it was just a bad decision. Stick all of that thinking into your tool box so, when you are placed in a similar situation, you can make the best decision with the information you have in the time allotted. Be yourself.

We all have leaders we look up to and want to be like. Ask yourself why you like them and try to emulate their traits, instead of the leaders themselves. I like them because they allow their subordinates to have and run with ideas. I like them because they communicate their vision clearly. I like them because they see problems coming before they become a crisis. Those are all things you can emulate. You have to be yourself or you will not be anybody.

How can you expect people to follow you if they do not know who you are? How can they know who you are if you do not know who you are? Figure yourself out first, then start leading others. If needed, rip off that tie and whistle and lead from the heart.

HOW TO MAKE IT A PRIORITY:
Evaluate yourself using evidence. What are you good at? What are you not good at? Be honest in your self-assessment by using evidence. What does the evidence say you are good at? It is easy to think we are good or bad at something, but sometimes we are the hardest to convince of our accolades and shortcomings.

At times I feel like a failure as a teacher, coach, husband, and father, but when I look for evidence I find very little. I know I am a terrible speller. The red underlines that show up every time I type an email or text are my evidence. I like to say this phrase when an eighth grader tells me something I do not believe or I know to be false: Prove it. It is a phrase you can use on yourself when you are brave enough to do that self-evaluation.

LESSON 1: EXPLOIT THE TALENT AROUND YOU

You are the leader, right? Lead the strengths of the people around you. I have seen leaders that refuse to give up knowledge or power. Most of them are really smart, but by keeping all the decisions at their level they are doing three things. First, they are owning the decisions they make, which is good. Second, they are not leveraging the talent of their subordinate leaders. Third, they are not being a leader. To be a leader, you need to leverage the talents of your subordinate leaders.

An example of this was illustrated to me in Latvia. The Latvian military leadership is loosely based on the Russian military. They have officers and workers and little to no middle management. I was talking with a Latvian platoon leader who was in charge of about 25 Soldiers. He was the only one allowed to make decisions. Watching the men work, it was obvious that one of the Soldiers was a leader, keeping everyone working, cracking jokes, and leading the group. In the American Army, this man would have been a subordinate leader, trusted with leading a small group within the vision of the senior leader. The idea was foreign to the Latvians. There was one leader who made all the decisions, everyone else just followed orders. That was it.

Flip to the exploitation of talents around you. My First Sergeant had already completed 31 years in the Army between the National Guard and active duty. He had been to Bosnia, Iraq, and now Afghanistan. There was nothing he had not seen, heard, or done himself. His talent was knowing people and organizing things. Some first sergeants are very aggressive and forceful in their job, mine was not. That was not his strength. However, when given a task or problem, he was a genius.

He was my number one go-to guy when it came to personal problems and he was instrumental in solving them and getting the best result. Awards ceremony? He used a sand table rehearsal and a walk-through rehearsal. He was so good at those two things. He took a lot of ownership of those tasks because his opinion was valued.

In school, it is much the same, except the talent around you might be other teachers or even students. What are they good at? Find it and use it! A lot of times students do not have any idea what they are good at, so it is up to the adult in the room to figure it out and convince them of it. I like to find students who are good at being friendly and helpful and place them near students who may be shy or need a little extra help. The friendly students can usually get the shy students to step out of their comfort zone little by little because of their sincerity. They can also help the students who need it because of their willingness to help and their empathy. I try to be careful with this too because I do not want my friendly students to be taken advantage of, they also need someone to be friendly and helpful to them. It is a balance, but when you find it, you can get back to that 2+2=5 type of math. If you have people around you, find out what their talents are, and exploit them. It gives them some ownership and makes them a part of the team.

HOW TO MAKE IT A PRIORITY:

Before you can prioritize talent, you must first recognize it and assess it. When assessing talent, you need to not only recognize what you think a person is good at, but also what they think they are good at. Most people know what they are good at. Take those strengths and multiply them! Do not let the fish on your team struggle to climb a tree when they can do all the swimming!

LESSON 1: GO TO WAR WITH THE ARMY YOU HAVE

Donald Rumsfeld was the 13th Secretary of Defense under President Gerald Ford (1975-1977) and the 21st Secretary of Defense under President George W. Bush (2001-2006). Rumsfeld once said of war, "You go to war with the army you have, not the army you might want or wish to have at a later time."

This is a quote that not only applies to going into a hostile Iraq with an outdated Army in both tactics and equipment, but about leading any organization. This can be applied to your family, church, or department at work. There are ways to make institutional changes, but you have to operate with what you have, not with what you do not. Great leaders can get more from their subordinates because they operate as a team and do more collectively than they could as a sum of their individual efforts.

This is never more true than on a high school football team. Come Friday night, you are on the field with the team you have. Someone might be hurt, academically ineligible, or sick. That does not stop the opening kickoff. So what do you do about it? You train your team to win. Sometimes you can get people in the best spot to make the team successful and sometimes you are just trying to survive another down. Either way, you are in a fight with the army you have.

In college and professional leagues coaches can recruit their army, but they are in the same boat when it comes time to take the field. They have to do their best with what they have, no excuses. At that level excuses will get a coach fired. They can make excuses or they can make football players.

The classroom is no different. We can only move as fast as we can move. Some classes can do a lot of extra things to expand their thinking on the material. Other classes are just trying to get through the material with a C minus average. In the public school setting, there is no changing the team you have, it is a matter of making the best of what you have. Every student can be good at something, it is the teacher's job to figure out what that is and exploit the heck out of it. The same could be said in any organization. (See Lesson 1: Exploit the talent around you.)

The best thing about this lesson is that you are always prepared for the worst. You are able to shift your thinking to a place where you believe, and get your followers to believe, there is always a way to be successful. With that mindset, you and your team can do astonishing things. Take that mindset and get a shot in the arm with a good player who moves to town from another state, or a grant that places tablets in every student's hand. You were prepared to move forward with what you had, but now you have more!

Put yourself on the follower's side of the equation. Is the person leading you always wishing they had more or are they placing all their effort in the current team? If you are a part of the team that the boss thinks is not good enough, how will you react? You may start to think you are not good enough. On the other hand, if your leader is pushing you to be the best and placing success on the shoulders of the current team, you will raise your level of performance to match.

There was a basketball coach here in the U.P. who would do just that. He was at a small school with maybe only 12 players on the team. He had five starters, but very quickly substituted in numbers six, seven, eight, nine, and ten. Part way through the second quarter he might have two of his top five and numbers six, eight, and ten on the floor. There was always a rotation, and everyone was making a maximum contribution to the team.

This did a few things for him. First, his top five players were always fresh. Even a 30 or 60 second rest is enough to recover. Second, his substitutes were used to playing with the top five. They were not as fast or as talented, but their level of play skyrocketed because it had to. When you play with the best, you become better. The third thing it did was allow his team to come together as a tight knit group. Every member of the team was valuable to the organization.

Counter this method with what we sometimes see at the end of a high school basketball game. One team is winning by a lot, and both teams send in their players that are not quite as talented or experienced. You see traveling, air-balls, and massive mistakes. I never saw the coach I mentioned above do this. He had a team that he went to war with every Tuesday and Thursday night.

Do you want to follow a boss who is always complaining about not having all they want or do you want to follow an innovative, optimistic leader?

HOW TO MAKE IT A PRIORITY:

Stop making excuses. Stop hoping for different people. If this is an issue for you, make a list of your people and write a strength next to each of their names. Ask them what their strength is, play to their strengths and their weaknesses will naturally improve. You can either own your situation and make the best of what you have, or you can complain about it and sabotage your own organization.

LESSON 1: KNOW WHEN TO TALK AND KNOW WHEN TO WRITE

I learned this lesson while working full time for the Army. If you do not want people to overreact or if you want to test the viability of something you are not sure is within regulations, make a phone call. You can get a lot done with a phone call without maintaining a written record. If you bounce your idea off of someone and determine that it is not feasible, then you can quickly move on. You can always follow up a phone call with an email, but once an email is out there, it is impossible to take back.

If you want something documented, start with a written record. A lot of things are done with email and text, and if it is out there, now you have a digital record of the communication. This can be used to your advantage when something goes wrong or happens at a different time. Countless times in the Army things are delayed or not accomplished to a certain standard and whoever is left answering to the boss has some explaining to do. I have been there many times, standing in front of an angry Lieutenant Colonel and pleading my case, just hoping they tell me to "GET OUT!" so I can go fix it. That conversation goes much better when two things are present. First, a plan to make it right. I am talking about an air-tight, no-frills, execute-now type of plan. The second thing that helps the conversation is a record of work. Sometimes you need those printed out emails to cover your backside.

Let us talk about the Reply All function in email for a second. I have seen Reply All completely devastate the Michigan National Guard email servers. One person wanted off of the distribution list, so they selected Reply All and asked to be removed from that email thread. That single email started a chain reaction of several people selecting Reply All and doing the same thing. Because it was not my job to deal with it, this situation was hilarious. It was a huge issue that has since been fixed, but something so simple as "Please do not send me these emails anymore," became a massive headache. With that said, Reply All should be used sparingly, in small or collaborative groups.

On a more serious note, unfortunately as leaders, we are sometimes forced to discipline our subordinates. This is the worst part of being a leader. However, this is an issue that must be documented. In my second company command, I was forced to fire a platoon leader because they were incompetent at their job. I documented this on developmental counseling forms at first, and then I asked for some guidance from a really great mentor of mine.

His advice, "Bury him." What he meant by that was to test his leadership by evaluating and documenting everything, good, bad, or ugly. The thought process was he will either rise to the occasion or be crushed by failure. He was crushed.

I did not set this leader up for failure, I set him up for success by giving him feedback after every mission. On some things he did okay, and on some things he failed miserably. The final straw was during a convoy back to our armory. He went through the Troop Leading Procedures with the help of another leader, and had put together a plan. The plan was not very well thought out or briefed, but he was showing improvement.

TROOP LEADING PROCEDURES: An

efficient and systematic way to plan, prepare, and execute missions. Steps: Receive the mission, Issue a warning order, Make a tentative plan, Initiate movement, Conduct reconnaissance, Complete the plan, Issue the operations order, Supervise and Refine.

The following morning at 4:30 am, my First Sergeant and I walked out to make sure everything was going okay. It was not. My platoon leader was nowhere to be found. The HMMWV's were lined up and ready to go, kind of. I tracked down a staff sergeant, who was not a squad leader, in the platoon moving the trucks back to the armory. He informed me that the platoon leader was not in his room and was not answering his phone. I took him aside and said, "I need you to take charge of this and get these trucks home. They have to leave on time." He replied, "Yes, Sir. Mission brief will be in 15 minutes." I do not remember the reasons that platoon leader gave me for not being where he was supposed to be, but it was not good. The trucks got back to the Armory just fine. The young staff sergeant that led the convoy was a trusted leader who was with me in Iraq and I knew the mission would be accomplished while he was in charge.

HMMWV: High Mobility Multi Wheeled Vehicle. The basic light tactical Army vehicle that replaced the Jeep in 1984. Commonly referred to as a HUM-V or HUMMER.

When I initially went to my boss about getting a new platoon leader he was not happy. This was not the first time he had heard about this particular leader's shortcomings, but the gap between being unhappy with a leader's performance and kicking them off the team is one that needs to be bridged with paperwork. Due to my mentor's suggestions, I had it. I could show, in writing, that he was incompetent at teaching, leading, assessing, and operating. Once my boss had this documentation in his hands, it was almost impossible to let him go with us to Afghanistan. It was clear I needed someone new and it was able to happen quickly due to my diligence in the documentation.

The same is true on the teacher's side of things. If a student did something to deserve detention or in-school suspension, it is fine to take the teacher's word for it, until it is not. When asked by an administrator or a parent, it is important to have something written down. It does not have to be fancy, but something so that you can speak intelligently about what happened. The same holds true in any organization. If punishment or reward is going to be based on an event, it is always better to have it written down.

HOW TO MAKE IT A PRIORITY:

There is one question you should ask to see which method you should use. If what I am about to put in this email were to be printed and placed on the bulletin board, or given to my boss, would it be okay? That might stop you right there. Electronic correspondence never goes away. You might delete it, but that does not mean it is gone. Thank you, screenshot function! Maybe the digital record is the reason you want to send your message via email or text, but put some thought into it first.

CLOSING

Leadership is an ever-changing dynamic that brings with it new, exciting, and sometimes impossible challenges. Being a leader means being the point person on the leading edge of those challenges. You are the first one to take the blame and the last one to get the credit. If you are a selfish leader you will not have followers for very long.

I could not possibly write a book that would tell you how to be successful in your unique situation, but I do believe you can help yourself by understanding some of these guiding principles when it comes to leadership. Some days (hours, minutes, moments), some of these Lessons will be at the front of your mind, on a slide in a board meeting, or talked about openly while other Lessons fall to the rear. In the next moment, one of those may be brought into the limelight. It is up to you to stay nimble and keep your leadership toolbox open and be bold when digging around for the right Lesson to apply at the right time, with the right people, in the right place.

Each Lesson is labeled as Lesson 1 because it is impossible to rank these in an analytical way for your job or situation. They cannot be ranked, but they can be prioritized based on your schedule. The beauty of identifying these Lessons based on your day is that it allows you to leverage leadership at different levels.

As you become more nimble in transitioning from one Lesson to another, you will find yourself becoming more specific and efficient in your leadership skills. This is a process, not a product, so treat it as such and try to be a better leader when you place your head on the pillow than you were when you picked it up.

You can phase these lessons into your life. At first, maybe you identify one lesson you will use in the morning, and one in the evening. After that, maybe you break the morning up into time at home and time at work. Next, maybe you start breaking up your time at work based on tasks.

Once you have a schedule built, start plugging in the Lesson(s) you will use during that time. Eventually, you will improve at blocking off time and scheduling it appropriately. You do not have to plan everything down to the minute. Some things might warrant this, while others just require a rough block of time. By mentally assigning a leadership Lesson to each block on your schedule, you will find yourself being more efficient with your time, with your coworkers, and with task completion. The progression of your schedule might look like this:

	Morning at Home	Morning at Home	Morning at Home
Morning	Morning at work	First tasks at work	
		Morning at work	Meeting with team
			Conference call
Afternoon	Afternoon at work	Afternoon at work	Proposal writing
			Meeting with boss
		Last tasks at work	Dinner with friends
	Evening	Relaxing	Read Lesson 1

Eventually, you will be transitioning between these 21 leadership leveraging principals with ease. You will be leveraging leadership in everyday life.

WORKS CITED

Meyer, U., & Coffey, W. R. (2017). Above the line: Lessons in leadership and life from a championship season. Penguin Books.

Paramount Pictures. (1991). Necessary roughness [DVD]. United States.

Touchstone Pictures. (1997). Con Air [DVD]. United States.

Tzu, S. (1991). The art of war. (T. Cleary, Trans.). Shambala.

Universal. (1985). Back to the future [DVD]. United States.

Warner Bros. (1986). Heartbreak Ridge [DVD]. United States.

ABOUT THE AUTHOR

John was born into a Navy family and attended eight different schools while crisscrossing the country. After graduating high school, John went to Northern Michigan University where he earned a degree in Elementary Education while serving in the Michigan Army National Guard and completing ROTC requirements to become a second lieutenant.

Upon graduation, John served as a military police and infantry platoon leader in Baghdad, Iraq. When he returned, he began his teaching and coaching career while continuing with the military.

John is currently an 8th grade U.S. History teacher in Kingsford, Michigan where he also enjoys coaching football and being involved in his church along with his wife and son. He is also an instructor in the Army reserves where he teaches Army Majors masters level courses as part of their professional military education.

In his free time, you can often find John hanging out with his wife or trekking through the woods, riding his four-wheeler, or taking the boat out enjoying nature with his son.

MORE FROM ROAD TO AWESOME

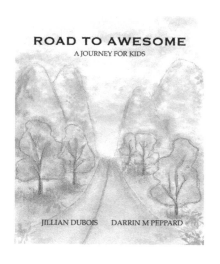

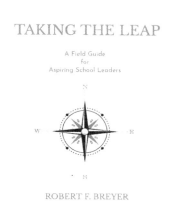

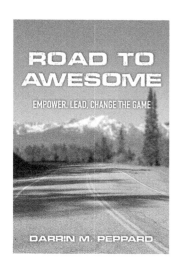

(Via Codebreaker)